Another Jesus

By
Allen Roesch

TEACH Services, Inc.
P U B L I S H I N G
www.TEACHServices.com • (800) 367-1844

Copyright © 2019 TEACH Services, Inc.
ISBN-13: 978-1-57258-322-3 (Paperback)
Library of Congress Control Number: 2005924144

Published by:

TEACH Services, Inc.
P U B L I S H I N G
www.TEACHServices.com • (800) 367-1844

Contents

Chapter 1

"...ANOTHER JESUS"

"I fear, lest by any means, as the serpent beguiled Eve through his subtlety, so your minds should be corrupted from the simplicity that is in Christ. For if he that cometh preacheth another Jesus, whom we have not preached...ye might well bear with him."   *{II Corinthians 11:3, 4}*

Is there any possibility whatsoever that large numbers of conservative, Spirit of Prophecy loving Seventh-day Adventists have, unbeknown to them, accepted 'another Jesus'?

Before you give your answer, consider a few facts.

We are told that there are more than a hundred million angels before the throne of God:

> "And I heard the voice of many angels round about the throne and the beasts and the elders (4 beasts & 24 elders, v.8) and the number of them was ten thousand times ten thousand, and thousands of thousands."
>
> {Revelation 5:11; See Daniel 7:10 also}

We are also told:

> "His false representations won to his side one-third of all the heavenly angels; and so strong was their delusion that they would not be corrected; they clung to Lucifer, and were expelled from Heaven with him."
>
> {*Signs of the Times*, October 25, 1883}

Even using the most conservative figures, of more than fifty million angels it is written: 'so strong was their delusion that they would not be corrected.' Incredible and sad beyond human comprehension. Fifty million angels, that for who knows how

1

long lived in the very presence of God; fifty million angels, who were free from the weaknesses and encumbrances of fallen humanity; deceived, so powerfully and horribly deceived, 'that they would not be corrected,' and were forever 'expelled from Heaven.'

How do we compare with angels? Well, originally not too bad: *"Thou madest him a little lower than the angels"* {Hebrews 2:7}. Unfortunately, things did not stay that way for long:

> "Man was originally endowed with noble powers and a well-balanced mind. He was perfect in his being, and in harmony with God. His thoughts were pure, his aims holy. But through disobedience, his powers were perverted, and selfishness took the place of love. His nature became so weakened through transgression that it was impossible for him, in his own strength, to resist the power of evil. He was made captive by Satan, and would have remained so forever had not God specially interposed."
>
> {*Steps to Christ* 17}

From there, for the most part, it has been nothing but downhill:

> "For four thousand years the race had been decreasing in physical strength, in mental power, and in moral worth."
>
> {*Desire of Ages* 117}

So far as our part of the equation is concerned, there can be no denying that the possibility of our being deceived must be almost infinitely greater than was that of the angels. And to make matters worse, not only has our ability to discern and resist the devil greatly decreased, but the devil's power to deceive has greatly increased:

> "The power of Satan now to tempt and deceive is ten-fold greater than it was in the days of the apostles. His power has increased, and it will increase, until it is taken away. His wrath and hate grow stronger as his time to work draws near its close."　　　　{*II Spiritual Gifts* 277}

"...ANOTHER JESUS"

'...ten-fold greater...and it will increase...His wrath and hate grow stronger.' We need a much deeper awareness of just how real (*"Satan does not merely pretend. He is in earnest."* 2T 287) and unceasing (*"An unceasing, desperate conflict between good and evil."* RH 5/3/06) this great controversy between good and evil is, which every one of us is a part of.

Surely, when we consider our weakness, along with Satan's tremendous power, it should cause us to realize to the very depths of our being: WE NEED GOD! And: WE NEED HIS WORD!

"...the word of life."   {Philippians 2:16}

"...the word of truth."   {Ephesians 1:13}

"...as it is in truth, the word of God."
                    {I Thessalonians 2:13}

"...the word, which is able to save your souls."
                    {James 1:21}

How was it that Satan managed to deceive so many heavenly beings?

"[Lucifer] sought to gain control of heavenly beings, to draw them away from their Creator, and to win their homage to himself. Therefore he misrepresented God... With his own evil characteristics he sought to invest the loving Creator. Thus he deceived angels."
                    {*Desire of Ages* 21, 22}

'He misrepresented God...Thus he deceived angels.' Satan deceived fifty million angels by presenting to them a wrong conception of the Father.

Not only is it possible, but it is a reality, that today Satan is deceiving multitudes of Seventh-day Adventists by presenting to them a wrong conception of the Son. In other words: 'another Jesus'.

ANOTHER JESUS

I feel I must sound two very solemn warnings in connection with what I just said. #1—This time it is not those poor, deluded 'Seventh-Day Adventists' that have given up their faith in the Spirit of Prophecy that it is happening to. #2—Few seem to realize just how serious and just how widespread this problem actually is.

Chapter 2

"THE TESTIMONY OF JESUS"

I know that many of you are anxious to hear my explanation of precisely how it is that Satan has succeeded in deceiving even conservative Adventists on this crucial subject. But before I do that I feel I need to spend some time (the next three chapters) on another subject. A subject that is possibly more important than any other: the exact place that God designs the Spirit of Prophecy to occupy in the life of every true Seventh-day Adventist.

In this chapter all I want to do is emphasize the importance of the Spirit of Prophecy.

M. L. Andreason once wrote:

> "In my more than sixty years of official connection with the denomination, one of my chief aims has been to inspire confidence in the Spirit of Prophecy. The last two years I have spoken on the subject 204 times."
>
> {*Letters to the Churches* 42, 43}

Ellen White herself tells us:

> "As the end draws near and the work of giving the last warning to the world extends, it becomes more important for those who accept present truth to have a clear understanding of the nature and influence of the Testimonies, which God in His providence has linked with the work of the third angel's message from its very rise."
>
> {*5 Testimonies* 654}

She also tells us:

> "In ancient times God spoke to men by the mouth of prophets and apostles. In these days He speaks to them by

5

the testimonies of His Spirit. There was never a time when God instructed His people more earnestly than He instructs them now concerning His will and the course that He would have them pursue." {*5 Testimonies* 661}

I question whether it is possible for us to ever fully appreciate the greatness of the truth contained in that last sentence; I do not question the blessedness of trying.

I want to make a few comparisons. They involve the work of three of the greatest, holiest men that ever walked this earth, compared to the work of Ellen White.

Person #1—Moses, the man of whom it is written:

"Moses was fitted to take pre-eminence among the great of the earth, to shine in the courts of its most glorious kingdom, and to sway the scepter of its power. His intellectual greatness distinguishes him above the great men of all ages. As historian, poet, philosopher, general of armies, and legislator, he stands without a peer."
{*Patriarchs and Prophets* 246}

"God blessed his ready obedience, and he became eloquent, hopeful, self-possessed, and well fitted for the greatest work ever given to man."
{*Patriarchs and Prophets* 255}

"Moses did not merely think of God, he saw Him. God was the constant vision before him. Never did he lose sight of His face." {*Education* 63}

"Moses, the holiest of men."
{*Signs of the Times*, November 10, 1881}

"There arose not a prophet since in Israel like unto Moses, whom the LORD knew face to face."
{Deuteronomy 34:10}

"THE TESTIMONY OF JESUS"

This incredible man Moses, who went up into the mount with God to receive the Ten Commandments, who stood in the place of God to His people, wrote five very small books (six when you include the book of Job). Ellen White wrote over a hundred books; many of them over twice the size of all those books of Moses combined. Consider another wonderful fact: those few small books by Moses were to guide God's people for thousands of years. That multitude of books from the pen of Ellen White were all written for the time of the end.

Person #2—John, the man of whom it is written:

"The one who most fully reflected the likeness of the Saviour..." {*Steps to Christ* 73}

"...His best-loved disciple." {*Desire of Ages* 146}

"...by association with Christ, the Great Teacher, he obtained the highest education which mortal man can receive." {*Sanctified Life* 61}

"The epistles of John breathe the spirit of love. It seems as if he wrote with a pen dipped in love." {*Acts of the Apostles* 554}

"...John, the recorder of the most sublime truths of the gospel." {Introduction of *Great Controversy*, first page}

This wonderful man, who most fully reflected the likeness of the Saviour, who recorded the most sublime truths of the gospel with a pen dipped in love: wrote well under fifty thousand words. Ellen White wrote over twenty-five million.

Person #3—Paul, the man of whom it is written:

"...except Him who spoke as never man spake, the most illustrious teacher that this world has known." {*Education* 51}

ANOTHER JESUS

"He had that greatest of all wisdom..."   {*Education* 66}

"There never lived a more self-denying, persevering worker."   {*Acts of the Apostles* 367}

"No man ever lived who was a more earnest, energetic, and self-sacrificing disciple of Christ than was Paul. He was one of the world's greatest teachers. He crossed the seas and traveled far and near, until a large portion of the world had learned from his lips the story of the cross of Christ."
{*4 Testimonies* 409}

"I am Jesus...I have appeared unto thee for this purpose, to make thee a minister."   {Acts 26:15, 16}

This most dedicated of all Christians, this greatest of human teachers, this man who wrote more books of the New Testament than all of the other New Testament writers combined: wrote approximately a hundred and twenty pages. Ellen White wrote over a hundred thousand pages.

I cannot even begin to adequately describe the greatness of the gift that God has given to us in the Spirit of Prophecy. Surely God, through His holy prophets, can do an infinitely better job describing it than I can:

"Behold, what manner of love the Father hath bestowed upon us."   {I John 3:1}

"This is the LORD'S doing; it is marvelous in our eyes."
{Psalms 118:23}

"What could have been done more to my vineyard, that I have not done in it?"   {Isaiah 5:4}

"How shall we escape, if we neglect so great salvation?"
{Hebrews 2:3}

"THE TESTIMONY OF JESUS"

Please, pray that you will realize more fully than ever before, that the Spirit of Prophecy truly is: 'the testimony of Jesus.'

Chapter 3

"...SO MANY WARNINGS"

I need to quickly go through a few basic truths:

#1—Mankind was created perfect.

#2—Through sin he became anything but perfect.

#3—"It was [Christ's] mission to bring to men complete restoration." {*Ministry of Healing* 17}

Unlike Calvinists, Seventh-Day Adventists believe that in this mission to bring to men complete restoration there is a:

> "...divine principle of co-operation, without which no true success can be attained." {*Prophets and Kings* 487}

> "In everything that tends to the sustenance of man is seen the concurrence of divine and human effort...Thus it is in spiritual things, in the formation of the character, and in every line of Christian work. We have a part to act, but we must have the power of divinity to unite with us, or our efforts will be in vain." {*Christ's Object Lessons* 82}

> "No one, not even God, can carry us to heaven unless we make the necessary effort on our part." {*5 Testimonies* 345}

God does His part and we must do our part. In this chapter I want to look at one particular aspect of this.

One major part in God's work to save mankind, second only to the gift of Jesus Christ Himself, is His giving to us the Bible. It is of supreme importance in God's plan to save us; and as such we should value it accordingly. Unquestionably, one of its most important and fundamental passages is II Timothy 3:16, 17:

"...SO MANY WARNINGS"

"All scripture is given by inspiration of God, and is profitable for doctrine, for reproof, for correction, for instruction in righteousness: That the man of God may be perfect, thoroughly furnished unto all good works."

{II Timothy 3:16, 17}

It is worthy of our utmost consideration that two of the first three things stated as the means through which the man of God may be made perfect are reproof and correction. The New Living Bible expresses it in these words:

"All Scripture is inspired by God and is useful to teach us what is true *and to make us realize what is wrong in our lives. It straightens us out* and teaches us to do what is right."

{II Timothy 3:16, 17 NLT}

This is an element of the plan of salvation, the importance of which, and the necessity of which, we cannot afford to underestimate or reject. Unfortunately, this is precisely what the vast majority of God's professed people have always been prone to do.

There have ever been two groups among God's professed people. (I say that in a very general sense.) The first, and by far the larger group, are those described in the book of Isaiah:

"[They] say to the seers, See not; and to the prophets, Prophesy not unto us right things, speak unto us smooth things, prophesy deceits."   {Isaiah 30:10}

Group number two, that very small remnant, are those who say with Jeremiah:

"O Lord, correct me."   {Jeremiah 10:24}

Before going on, I think it is important that I try to show that many people fall somewhere between group one and group two. They hear and accept some of God's corrections, but reject others; which eventually, and inevitably, will result in their being 'left behind':

11

"AN IMPRESSIVE DREAM"

"While at Battle Creek in August, 1868, I dreamed of being with a large body of people...As we journeyed, the road seemed to ascend...As we journeyed on, the road grew narrower and steeper...As we progressed, the path still continued to grow narrow...As the path grew more narrow...The path finally became so narrow...

"We then thought of those who had not accustomed themselves to privations and hardships. Where were such now? They were not in the company. At every change some were left behind, and those only remained who had accustomed themselves to endure hardships. The privations of the way only made these more eager to press on to the end."

{*2 Testimonies* 594, 595}

'At every change some were left behind': which tells us, many traveled for some distance and some length of time on the ever narrowing road, making the necessary changes and giving up whatever it was that God revealed needed to be given up; but at some point, for some reason, they said with those disciples of Christ in John chapter six, 'now you're asking too much,' and like them, they 'walked with Him no more.' (verses 60, 66) A horribly sad and solemn warning indeed!

Two more particulars of this dream deserve to be emphasized before going on. The first is the fact that from beginning to end the path grew narrower and narrower. Is the path we are traveling on growing narrower and narrower? If not, then we need to do some real heart searching. We should strive to keep ever in our minds these words of Him who has traveled the path before us:

"Enter ye in at the strait gate: for wide is the gate, and broad is the way, that leadeth to destruction, and many there be which go in thereat: Because strait is the gate, and narrow is the way, which leadeth unto life, and few there be that find it."   {Matthew 7:13, 14}

"...SO MANY WARNINGS"

"Strive to enter in at the strait gate: for many, I say unto you, will seek to enter in, and shall not be able."

{Luke 13:24}

The second point that needs to be emphasized is brought out in these two sentences:

#1—"Those who had not accustomed themselves to privations and hardships...were left behind."
#2—"Those *only* remained who had accustomed themselves to endure hardships."   {*2 Testimonies* 595}

Now, back to where I was: the place of reproof and correction in God's plan for our salvation; which brings me to the title of this chapter: '...so many warnings.' These, as you probably already realize, are the last three words of a quote from the Spirit of Prophecy. Do you know what the rest of the quote says? Before telling you, let me say a few words. Philippians 2:5 tells us: "*Let this mind be in you, which was also in Christ Jesus.*" I hope we would all agree, that if anyone had the mind of Christ, Ellen White did. We need to seek with all our heart for that kind of experience; and when we have it, we will then say with her:

"I have been looking over the Testimonies given for Sabbathkeepers and I am astonished at the mercy of God and His care for His people in giving them *so many warnings.*"   {*5 Testimonies* 662}

When our hearts are truly right with God, and we see things as they really are, we will know and understand that God's warnings, as well as His reproofs and corrections, are just as much a part of His love, and just as much a part of His plan for our salvation as anything else He has said or done; and for us the words will become more and more true, "*...the wise, when rebuked will love you all the more.*" {Prov. 9:8 NLT} This does not come naturally, nor does it come easily. But come it must if we are to truly walk that ever narrowing path.

ANOTHER JESUS

In chapter two I cited this quote:

> "As the end draws near and the work of giving the last warning to the world extends, it becomes more important for those who accept present truth to have a clear understanding of the nature and influence of the Testimonies, which God in His providence has linked with the work of the third angel's message from its very rise."
>
> {5 *Testimonies* 654}

I fear that most of us don't 'have a clear (enough) understanding' of just how large (and important) a part of the Testimonies consists of warnings, reproofs, and corrections. Along with that, I fear that most of us don't 'have a clear (enough) understanding' of just how true it is, that '*the destiny of [every one of us] hangs*' {EW 270} on how we receive these warnings, reproofs, and corrections.

I believe the quotes that I am about to share with you are not only just as blessed, and just as wonderful, as her most inspiring descriptions of the love of God, but in this one sense are even more needful: they bring to light her work as 'a reprover of His people', which is such a tremendous aid in our effort to accomplish this—"*unless you clear away the rubbish that keeps the Lord Jesus out, He cannot possibly enter.*" {This Day With God 74}

> "There are some in these last days who will cry: 'Speak unto us smooth things, prophesy deceits.' But this is not my work. God has set me as a reprover of His people...I have not chosen this unpleasant labor for myself. It is not a work which will bring to me the favor or praise of men. It is a work which but few will appreciate." {5 *Testimonies* 679}

> "My work has been to speak plainly of the faults and errors of God's people...I have been shown that it is not mine to choose my work, but humbly to obey the will of God. The errors and wrongdoings in the lives of professed Christians are recorded for the instruction of those who are liable to fall into the same temptations. The experience of

one serves as a beacon light to warn others off the rocks of danger.

"*Thus* are revealed the snares and devices of Satan, the importance of perfecting Christian character, and the means by which this result may be obtained. *Thus* God indicates what is necessary to secure His blessing. There is a disposition on the part of many to let rebellious feelings arise if their peculiar sins are reproved. The spirit of this generation is: "Speak unto us smooth things." But the spirit of prophecy speaks only the truth."   {*4 Testimonies* 13}

"I was shown that God has laid upon my husband and me a special work, to bear a plain testimony to His people, and to cry aloud and spare not, to show the people their transgressions and the house of Israel their sins…[Many] think that the labors of Brother and Sister White would be acceptable if they were not continually condemning wrong and reproving sin. I was shown that God has laid this work upon us."   {*3 Testimonies* 258-261}

"I have tried in the fear of God to set before His people their danger and their sins, and have endeavored, to the best of my feeble powers, to arouse them. I have stated startling things, which, if they had believed, would have caused them distress and terror, and led them to zeal in repenting of their sins and iniquities. I have stated before them that, from what was shown me, but a small number of those now professing to believe the truth would eventually be saved—not because they could not be saved, but because they would not be saved in God's own appointed way. The way marked out by our divine Lord is too narrow and the gate too strait to admit them while grasping the world or while cherishing selfishness or sin of any kind. There is no room for these things; and yet there are but few who will consent to part with them, that they may pass the narrow way and enter the strait gate."

{*2 Testimonies* 445, 446}

"Let none entertain the thought that I regret or take back any plain testimony I have borne to individuals or to the people. If I have erred anywhere, it is in not rebuking sin more decidedly and firmly."   {*5 Testimonies* 677}

I need to go just a little bit further before bringing this chapter to a close.

In the midst of those quotes, as well as throughout all the Testimonies, are statements like these:

"...from what was shown me, *but a small number* of those now professing to believe the truth would eventually be saved...*there are but few* who will consent to..."

{*2 Testimonies* 446}

"It is not a work which will bring to me the favor or praise of men. It is a work which *but few will appreciate*."

{*5 Testimonies* 679}

Because it was a work which but few appreciated, the life of Ellen White was at times made very hard and very sad:

"Painful though it has been to me, I have faithfully set before the offenders their faults and the means of remedying them."   {*5 Testimonies* 661}

"I seldom weep, but now I find my eyes blinded with tears; they are falling upon my paper as I write. It may be that erelong all prophesyings among us will be at an end, and the voice which has stirred the people may no longer disturb their carnal slumbers."   {*5 Testimonies* 77}

Almost a hundred years ago that voice which had stirred God's people for so many years was laid to rest. Today the name of Ellen White is held sacred among Seventh-day Adventists; and rightly so. But Jesus spoke a very solemn and unwelcome truth to those who professed to be God's people in His day; and it is a truth that we cannot pretend does not have an application today:

> "Woe unto you, scribes and Pharisees, hypocrites! Because ye build the tombs of the prophets, and garnish the sepulchres of the righteous. And say, If we had been in the days of our fathers, we would not have been partakers with them in the blood of the prophets…" {Matthew 23:29, 30}

Every one of us need to closely *"examine ourselves to see if we (truly) be in the faith."* {II Cor.13:5} and *"walk in the light and encourage others to follow our example."* {*Great Controvery* 598}

I would like to finish this chapter with two wonderfully encouraging quotes; one from the Spirit of Prophesy, the other from the Bible:

> "Jesus with solemn tenderness explained the purpose of the husbandman. The pruning will cause pain, but it is the Father who applies the knife." {*Desire of Ages* 677}

> "I am no longer sorry that I sent that letter to you, though I was sorry for a time, for I know that it was painful to you for a little while. Now I am glad I sent it, not because it hurt you, but because the pain caused you to have remorse and change your ways. It was the kind of sorrow God wants his people to have, so you were not harmed by us in any way. For God can use sorrow in our lives to help us turn away from sin and seek salvation. For godly sorrow worketh repentance to salvation. We will never regret that kind of sorrow." {II Corinthians 7:8-10 NLT, KJV}

Chapter 4

"...DOWN TO THE MINUTIAE"

As the path in the dream grew more and more narrow, so our understanding of God's word and its application to our lives must correspondingly come closer and closer to home. But before continuing down this narrowing road of truth I think it is important that a warning be sounded against going farther than God would intend.

While Satan is content to have the vast majority walk down the broad road, he is even more delighted to have some depart out of the broad road, cross over the narrow road, and end up in that most disgraceful of roads—fanaticism:

> "[Satan] would be better pleased to have fanatical persons embrace the testimony, and use it in his cause, than to have them remain in a lukewarm state."
>
> {*II Spiritual Gifts* 223} {*7 Bible Commentary* 962}

Having sounded that warning, let me continue down (I suppose it would be more in keeping with the vision to say up) this ever narrowing road. While what I am about to point out is certainly nothing new, I am convinced that for the vast majority of people—of all faiths—it is the great testing point. It can be expressed in one little word of supreme importance: ALL.

"He who hath an ear to hear, let him hear what the Spirit saith to the churches."

"God, who at sundry times and in divers manners spake in times past", this great truth of supreme importance, "unto the fathers by the prophets":

> "These be the words that **Moses** spake unto all Israel...if thou shalt seek the LORD thy God, thou shalt find him, if

18

thou seek him with all thy heart and with all thy soul."
{Deuteronomy 1:1; 4:29}

"Then **Joshua** said unto them…take diligent heed…to walk in all his ways, and to serve him with all your heart and with all your soul." {Joshua 22:1, 2, 5}

"And **Samuel** said unto the people…serve the LORD with all your heart." {I Samuel 12:20}

"And **Solomon**…said…walk before [Him] with all [your] heart." {I Kings 8:22, 23}

"Now these are the words of the letter that **Jeremiah** the prophet sent…thus saith the LORD…ye shall seek me, and find me, when ye shall search for me with all your heart."
{Jeremiah 29:1, 10, 13}

"The word of the LORD that came to **Joel**…thus saith the LORD, turn ye even to me with all your heart."
{Joel 1:1; 2:12}

"God, who at sundry times and in divers manners spake in time past unto the fathers by the prophets, hath in these last days spoken," this great truth of supreme importance, "unto us by His Son":

"…Master, which is the first commandment of all? Jesus answered him, The first of all the commandments is…thou shalt love the Lord thy God with all thy heart, and with all thy soul, and with all thy mind, and with all thy strength: this is the first and great commandment."
{Mark 12:29, 30; Matthew 22:36, 38}

As some of those Old Testament texts brought out, obeying God is inseparably connected with loving Him:

19

"If ye love me keep my commandments...He that hath my commandments, and keepeth them, he it is that loveth me." {John 14:15, 21}

"This is the love of God, that we keep His commandments." {I John 5:3}

Sadly, mankind has always been very slow to learn these lessons. But God, in His infinite love and wonderful patience, continues to teach them; this time through one whose words are both unmistakably clear and incredibly moving:

"True sanctification means perfect love, perfect obedience, perfect conformity to the will of God." {*Acts of the Apostles* 565}

"Look to Jesus, he is your pattern. Strive to have your lives as much like his as possible. Do not rest satisfied until you know that you love God with all your heart, and that his will is your will...O, get ready to meet your Lord in peace." {*Youth Instructor*, December 1, 1852}

Finally, I would like to present to you the paragraph containing the title of this chapter:

"One stood by my side and said: "God has raised you up and has given you words to speak to the people and to reach hearts as He has given to no other one...You must be unmoved by scorn, derision, reproach, and censure...The world abounds in testimonies given to please and charm for the moment, and to exalt self. Your testimony is of a different character. *It is to come down to the minutiae of life...*" {*2 Testimonies* 607, 608}

Rather than comment on that last quote, I would just like to ask you: before you continue on, please do some very serious heart searching concerning all that I have shared with you in these last few chapters. As I said at the beginning of them, I believe this question of the exact place that God designs the Spirit of Prophecy to occupy in the life (and heart) of every true Seventh-day Adventist is possibly more important than anything else. To a large degree, everything else is affected by this.

I would like to finish this section with one last quote. I want to preface it by saying: the Spirit of Prophecy tells us, *"All His promises, His warnings, are but the breathing of unutterable love."* {*SC* 35} This last quote contains both promises and warnings. Please, receive them for what they truly are, the breathing of unutterable love:

> "Those who are reproved by the Spirit of God should not rise up against the humble instrument. It is God, and not an erring mortal, who has spoken to save them from ruin. Those who despise the warning will be left in blindness to become self-deceived. But those who heed it, and zealously go about the work of separating their sins from them in order to have the needed graces, will be opening the door of their hearts that the dear Saviour may come in and dwell with them. This class you will ever find in perfect harmony with the testimony of the Spirit of God." {*3 Testimonies* 257}

Chapter 5

"OF ALL THE LESSONS TO BE LEARNED..."

I have chosen this quote (and subject) as the avenue by which to begin looking at this all-important question of whether or not many conservative Seventh-day Adventists have in fact accepted 'another Jesus'. The title of this chapter, as many of you probably recognize, is taken from the chapter in *Desire of Ages*—The Temptation:

> "Of all the lessons to be learned from our Lord's first great temptation none is more important than that bearing upon the control of the appetites and passions."
>
> {*Desire of Ages* 122}

I want to spend a few minutes on the subject of appetite, which will lead into the subject of passions. This, ultimately, will lead into the subject of the book.

Appetite is one of those areas where the Spirit of Prophecy comes down to the minutiae of life. Not many things come closer to home than this one. And as Ellen White informs us, none are more important.

Being somewhat simplistic, there are generally two ways that people tend to view the health message: a burden or a blessing. Not surprisingly, the Spirit of Prophecy has a word for both:

Those who look upon it as a burden

"When the requirements of God are accounted a burden because they cut across human inclination, we may know that the life is not a Christian life." (This quote gives cause for some real heart searching; and not just on the subject of appetite.)   {*Christ's Object Lessons* 97}

Those who look upon it as a blessing

"Lead them to study that marvelous organism, the human system, and the laws by which it is governed. Those who perceive the evidences of God's love, who understand something of the wisdom and beneficence of His laws, and the results of obedience, will come to regard their duties and obligations from an altogether different point of view. Instead of looking upon an observance of the laws of health as a matter of sacrifice or self-denial, they will regard it, as it really is, as an inestimable blessing."

{*Counsels on Diet and Foods* 457, 458}

Much could be brought out in regard to the importance of controlling the appetite, but since appetite is not really the subject of this book I will only share three quotes:

"Here is a work before you which will come closer and be more trying than anything which has yet been brought to bear upon you...You are stumbling over the very blessing which heaven has placed in your path to make progress less difficult. Satan presents this before you in the most objectionable light, that you may combat that which would prove the greatest benefit to you, which would be for your physical and spiritual health."

{*Counsel on Diet and Foods* 39}

"The controlling power of appetite will prove the ruin of thousands, when, if they had conquered on this point, they would have had moral power to gain the victory over every other temptation of Satan." {*3 Testimonies* 491, 492}

I would like to use this last quote as the connecting link between appetite and passion:

"A close sympathy exists between the physical and the moral nature. Any habit which does not promote health degrades the higher and nobler faculties...Indulgence of appetite strengthens the animal propensities, giving them the ascendancy over the mental and spiritual powers."

{Sanctified Life 25}

'Indulgence of appetite strengthens the animal propensities.' I would like to stop here and share something from my own experience. My wife and I have owned a health food store for almost ten years. Over those years we have held many cooking classes. Between the store and the cooking classes we (especially my wife) have met and talked with scores of people. One thing is absolutely certain: by a huge majority women are far more willing to give up their meat than men. We, as Seventh-day Adventists, should understand that meat eating and being carnal go hand-in-hand. Anyone who has been alive for any length of time should also know that as a rule men are more carnal than women. All of which leads me to what is a delicate but necessary statement.

My wife and I have discussed this subject, though not usually from this starting point, with many people. As with the number of women that are willing to give up meat eating, in comparison to men; similarly, we have found that women are generally far more likely to see the truth on this subject than men are. What I would like to say now, because of that, and I hope to say it in the most God fearing, solemn way I possibly can: all of you men who may initially be convinced that I am mistaken; please allow me to ask you to be willing to listen to the input of some woman (or women) that you have reason to believe is truly modest and spiritual; hopefully someone like your wife, or your sister, or your mother, or even your adult daughter. I also want to say, that if it is someone outside of your immediate family it should be done with the utmost propriety. We live in a very immoral and improper world, and Seventh-day Adventists need to set the highest example in this regard.

Let me say before starting, this whole subject covers a much broader area than where I am going to begin; actually, it is intimately connected with every aspect of life. I only wanted to begin in this way hoping that it would expose this deception in its clearest and most hideous form.

I want to share two quotes before beginning. They contain extremely important principles that need to be kept in mind as we examine this subject:

"OF ALL THE LESSONS TO BE LEARNED…"

"We are to look to the man Christ Jesus…He is the pattern man. His experience is the measure of the experience that we are to gain."　　　{ *7 Bible Commentary* 970}

"Man will never rise higher than his standard of purity or goodness or truth."　　　{ *Great Controversy* 555}

Finally, the long awaited moment.

I want to combine two very short Bible texts. Both share the word 'tempted'. (Chapter nine will be devoted to taking a closer look at what the Bible and Spirit of Prophecy teach in regard to 'temptation' and exactly what it means to be 'tempted.') The all-important questions are: does text #2 shed light on, and help us to better understand, text #1? Or: does combining text #2 with text #1 put the character and life of Christ in an all-together perverted light?

Text #1—"He was in all points tempted like as we are."
　　　{Hebrews 4:15}

Text #2—"Every man is tempted, when he is drawn away of his own lust."　　　{James 1:14}

For the remainder of this chapter I would like just to begin examining which of those two questions truthfully describes the relationship of text #2 to text #1. Then I would like to stop and try to lay some kind of a foundation for this whole subject. My aim is to try to keep this as short and as simple as possible.

Let me say before going on, hopefully many of you instantly see how horrible it is to apply text #2 to the experience of Christ; and therefore you may naturally be inclined to think: "This is no powerful deception that is going to fool many dedicated Seventh-day Adventists." Let me repeat what I said a few paragraphs back: what we are looking at right now is this teaching in its clearest and most hideous form. I assure you, it is usually presented in a much more subtle, and therefore, much less recognizable form. Along with that, it is oftentimes presented more in relation to our own experience than to Christ's, which also causes it to be much more likely to be accepted. I will be looking at this teaching in its broader form in a latter chapter.

In the Bible the word lust is often used in a much broader sense than just sexual desire (which I will also be spending more time on later), but there can be no denying that improper sexual desire is one of its primary meanings. And if ever there was a time when God's people needed to rightly understand this subject of lust, and even more importantly, be right in their hearts and souls concerning it, now is that time:

"Blessed are the pure in heart for they shall see God."

{Matthew 5:8}

"A terrible picture of the condition of the world has been presented before me. Immorality abounds everywhere. Licentiousness is the special sin of this age. Never did vice lift its deformed head with such boldness as now."

{2 *Testimonies* 346}

Those last words, though written over a hundred years ago, were never truer. Society continues to sink lower and lower, while at the same time human nature continues to grow weaker and weaker. This subject alone is a perfect example of why Ellen White said: 'I am astonished at the mercy of God and His care for His people in giving them so many warnings, pointing out their dangers':

"The Israelites, who could not be overcome by the arms or by the enchantments of Midian, fell a prey to her harlots. Such is the power that woman, enlisted in the service of Satan, has exerted to entrap and destroy souls. "She hath cast down many wounded: yea, many strong men have been slain by her." Proverbs 7:26. It was thus that the children of Seth were seduced from their integrity, and the holy seed became corrupt. It was thus that Joseph was tempted. Thus Samson betrayed his strength, the defense of Israel, into the hands of the Philistines. Here David stumbled. And Solomon, the wisest of kings, who had thrice been called the beloved of his God, became a slave of passion, and sacrificed his integrity to the same bewitching power.

"Now all these things happened unto them for ensamples: and they are written for our admonition, upon whom the ends of the world are come. Wherefore let him that thinketh he standeth take heed lest he fall." 1 Corinthians 10:11, 12. Satan well knows the material with which he has to deal in the human heart. He knows—for he has studied with fiendish intensity for thousands of years—the points most easily assailed in every character; and through successive generations he has wrought to overthrow the strongest men, princes in Israel, by the same temptations that were so successful at Baalpeor. All along through the ages there are strewn wrecks of character that have been stranded upon the rocks of sensual indulgence. As we approach the close of time, as the people of God stand upon the borders of the heavenly Canaan, Satan will, as of old, redouble his efforts to prevent them from entering the goodly land. He lays his snares for every soul."

{*Patriarchs and Prophets* 457}

Did Christ face this temptation?

"Those who have decided to obey the commandments of God will understand by experience that they have adversaries who are controlled by a power from beneath. Such adversaries beset Christ at every step, how constantly and determinedly no human being can ever know."

{*Christ's Object Lessons* 170}

"Satan was unwearied in his efforts to overcome the Child of Nazareth...His life was one long struggle against the powers of darkness...He left no means untried to ensnare Jesus." {*Desire of Ages* 71}

There can be only one answer to that question: Yes, Christ most certainly did face this temptation. Which brings us back to the all-important questions: Does text #2—"Every man is tempted, when he is drawn away of his own lust," shed light on, and help us to better understand text #1—"He was in all points tempted like as we are"? Or: Does combining text #2 with text #1 put the character and life of Christ in an all-together perverted light?

Again, what must ever be kept in mind in connection with this is:

"He is the pattern man. His experience is the measure of the experience that we are to gain."

{*7 Bible Commentary* 970}

"Man will never rise higher than his standard of purity or goodness or truth."   {*Great Controversy* 555}

Let me begin answering the question: Can the words, 'drawn away of his own lust', be correctly applied to the experience of Christ?

"The prince of this world cometh," said Jesus, "and hath nothing in Me." John 14:30. There was in Him nothing that responded to Satan's sophistry." {*Desire of Ages* 123}

Can those words, 'nothing that responded', be made to harmonize with those words, 'drawn away'?

"lust...[this] sinful emotion"   {*I Selected Messages* 217}

In this particular quote we are told that lust is a 'sinful emotion'. I cannot see how anyone could possibly believe that Christ, even for one second, had a sinful emotion. (I would encourage you to read this quote in its entirety.)

"Never lived there another who so hated evil."

{*Education* 79}

"Never before had there been a being upon the earth who hated sin with so perfect a hatred as did Christ."

{*I Selected Messages* 254}

How could someone lust after something they have a perfect hatred for? Try to think of just one thing in this entire world that you have a perfect hatred for. Do you find yourself lusting after it?

I came across this next quote during family worship this morning:

> "The youth may have principles so firm that the most powerful temptations of Satan will not draw them away from their allegiance." {*3 Testimonies* 472}

If it is true (which of course it is) that 'the youth may have principles so firm that Satan's most powerful temptations *will not draw them away*,' then it is absolutely horrible to teach that the Lord Jesus Christ, when tempted, *was drawn away*.

This next quote is Ellen White's in-depth look at the story of the woman that was caught in adultery (actually, she was lead into adultery by the Pharisees). She was then brought to Christ by those same Pharisees in an attempt to trap Him:

> "Jesus looked for a moment upon the scene—the trembling victim in her shame, the hard-faced dignitaries, devoid of even human pity. His spirit of stainless purity shrank from the spectacle...He stooped, and fixing His eyes upon the ground, began to write in the dust...There, traced before them, were the guilty secrets of their own lives...The accusers had been defeated. Now, their robe of pretended holiness torn from them, they stood, guilty and condemned, in the presence of Infinite Purity..."
> {*Desire of Ages* 461, 462}

In the midst of her account of the story, which has much more detail than I have included here, Ellen White makes, among others, two statements in reference to Christ:

> "His spirit of stainless purity shrank from the spectacle."

> "...they stood, guilty and condemned, in the presence of Infinite Purity."

Infinite Purity and lust; putting those two things together in the person of Christ seems about as unthinkable as putting light and darkness together:

> "Christ is light, and in Him is no darkness at all."
> {*Review & Herald*, April 7, 1904} {*Welfare Ministry* 79}

(Interestingly, Ellen White uses the exact same term to describe Christ—'Infinite Purity'—on page 37 of *Desire of Ages*; only this time it was before His incarnation.)

I would like to stop briefly and spend a little time (three short chapters) pointing out a few things in connection with this subject that I believe deserve some consideration.

As I close this chapter I do so with the realization that there are probably many of you out there that are still convinced that I am mistaken in my understanding of this subject of lust and temptation and James 1:14. To you I say, please read this final quote prayerfully and with an open mind. Please, ask God for the courage and humility to admit that you are wrong (the quote leaves room for only one conclusion). Also pray that you will truly see what a tremendous bearing our understanding of this text has on our entire Christian experience.

The brackets, and the words within the brackets, are not mine, but Ellen White's:

> "The rebellious purpose formed in the heart needs not expression by word or act to consummate the sin, and bring the soul into condemnation. The unlawful word or deed is but the fruition of the evil which has taken root in the heart; the outward evidence that temptation has prevailed, and hell has triumphed. Says the apostle, 'Every man is tempted [that is, enters into temptation] when he is drawn away of his own lust and enticed.'"
> {*Signs of the Times*, March 9, 1882}

Chapter 6

"THIS IS LIFE ETERNAL..."

The Spirit of Prophecy tells us:

"The great truths necessary for salvation are made as clear as noonday." {*Steps to Christ* 89}

It seems to me that there can hardly be a greater truth, which can be more necessary for salvation, than the truth expressed in these words of Christ Himself:

"This is life eternal, that they might know thee the only true God, and Jesus Christ whom thou hast sent." {John 17:3}

I thank God with all my heart, and believe it with all my heart, when He tells us, through the Spirit of Prophecy, that this great truth, which is so necessary for salvation, is made as clear as noonday. Satan may, and will, try with all his demonic might to confuse and pervert this great truth. False teachers, sincerely or otherwise, may, and will, try with all their might to confuse and pervert this great truth. Yet none of them will ever be able to change the fact that God has made this great truth as clear as noonday. But let it be realized, and never forgotten:

"In order to arrive at truth, we must have a sincere desire to know the truth and a willingness of heart to obey it." {*Steps to Christ* 111}

The Spirit of Prophecy, as is so often the case, clarifies and broadens our understanding of these great truths that God is trying to communicate to us through the Scriptures:

"Remember that a knowledge of God and of Christ is the sum of all science. God teaches us to count all things but loss for the excellency of the knowledge of Christ Jesus our Lord. To know God and Christ—this is eternal life. Incorporated with the life, this knowledge fits us for heaven."
{I Sermons and Talks 334}

"Paul saw that the character of Christ must be understood before men could love Him or view the cross with the eye of faith. Here must begin that study which shall be the science and the song of the redeemed through all eternity."
{Acts of the Apostles 273}

There is another 'great truth' that goes hand in hand with this 'great truth', and is just as much a motivating factor in the writing of this book as this 'great truth':

"The seal of the living God will be placed upon those only who bear a likeness to Christ in character."
{7 Bible Commentaries 970} {*Review & Herald,* May 21, 1895}

"…the only way to obtain an inheritance in the heavens is to become like Christ in character." {*Our High Calling* 72}

Those last three quotes not only all speak of Christ, but they also share one other word in common: character. We, as Seventh-day Adventists, are so very fortunate to have the Spirit of Prophecy to direct our attentions and energies in the right direction:

"Character building is the most important work ever entrusted to human beings; and never before was its diligent study so important as now." {*Education* 225}

Character building and knowing Christ; two subjects of supreme importance. And they are two subjects that must ever be combined. Let it never be forgotten, the first (character building) can never be undertaken successfully apart from the second (knowing Christ). And let it be realized as never before, that *"all the things thou canst desire are not to be compared unto [these]."* {Prov. 3:15} These two things are worth more than anything and everything this world has to offer. The fulfilling of these two things will make us a glory to God and a blessing to our fellow man. They will also bring true and eternal happiness.

The Spirit of Prophecy tells us: *"Merely to hear or to read the word is not enough. He who desires to be profited by the Scriptures must meditate upon the truth that has been presented to him."* {COL 59, 60} I believe that every quote in this chapter is worth meditating upon; and I would like to finish with a few more worth meditating upon. Please, don't just read them. Meditate upon them, memorize them, repeat them to yourself often, and determine to make them a living reality in your life.

CHARACTER BUILDING

"A good name is rather to be chosen than great riches."
{Proverbs 22:1}

"A character formed according to the divine likeness is the only treasure that we can take from this world to the next." {*Christ's Object Lessons* 332}

"When the character of Christ shall be perfectly reproduced in His people, then He will come to claim them as His own." {*Christ's Object Lessons* 69}

KNOWING CHRIST

"Grace and peace be multiplied unto you *through* the knowledge of God, and of Jesus our Lord, according as his divine power hath given unto us all things that pertain unto life and godliness, *through* the knowledge of Him."
{II Peter 1:2, 3}

ANOTHER JESUS

"We must know Christ personally. Then only can we rightly represent Him to the world."   { *6 Testimonies* 121}

"We can know Christ only by loving and obeying Him."
{ *Sons and Daughters of God* 205}

Chapter 7

"WHATSOEVER THINGS WERE WRITTEN..."

"Everything that was written in the past was written to teach us."
{Romans 15:4 from most modern translations}

One of those things that was 'written in the past' contains a lesson that is of the utmost importance with respect to our search for truth in regard to the subject of this book. To fail to be aware of this lesson and to give it the consideration it deserves can, and oftentimes does, result in a very serious wrong assumption being made.

In the days of Christ there were two major sides within the ministry of the church: the Pharisees and the Sadducees. One side was more conservative; the other side more liberal. One side (at least outwardly) tried to live by the law; the other side did not. One side was also more correct doctrinally. Both sides struggled for control of the 'church'. Both sides tried hard to influence the hearts and minds of the people. *Both sides were wrong.*

The parallels cannot be denied. Today there are two sides in the church and in the ministry of the church. One side is more conservative, the other side is more liberal. One side tries to live by both the Bible and Spirit of Prophecy, the other side not nearly so much. One side is definitely more correct doctrinally. Both sides have struggled for control of the church. Both sides also try very hard to influence the hearts and minds of the people.

To ignore or deny the possibility that both sides could also be wrong today would be ignoring and denying the lesson of Bible history. Failing to see this possibility leads to the logical (but dangerous) assumption that since it is clear that the one side is wrong (the liberal side), then the other side (the conservative side) must be right. This subject is too important to take any chance of making a wrong assumption. Please do not misunderstand me. I am not saying that both sides have to be wrong. I am only saying that this subject is far too important not to carefully consider the possibility. Remember: 'Everything that was written in the past was written to teach us.'

Though this book is concerned primarily with looking at the views of the conservative side, I still need to spend a few minutes examining and commenting on some of the views of the liberal side (generally termed "New Theology"). There are two things I hope to accomplish by doing this. First, I feel a need to try to make it as clear as possible that my views are not in harmony with those on the liberal side. The reason for this relates to the question that I've brought up as to the possibility that both sides could be wrong. Inevitably, when I state that I believe there are serious misunderstandings with many on the conservative side (on this specific subject), people tend to automatically assume that my views are more in harmony with those on the liberal side. Nothing could be further from the truth.

Since this study has everything to do with examining the experience of Christ, especially as our example of what it means to live a sinless life, I think it is crucial that I try to show that I am not in harmony with the New Theology when it comes to their understanding of the human nature of Christ. At the same time, I think this is a perfect opportunity to show how true it is that the New Theology is nothing short of open denial of what the Spirit of Prophecy clearly teaches:

> "He [Christ] took upon him our sinful nature."
> {*Review & Herald*, December 15, 1896}

> "He took upon His sinless nature our sinful nature..."
> {*Medical Ministry* 181}

> "In taking upon Himself man's nature in its fallen condition..."
> {*5 Bible Commentary* 1131}

In spite of quotes like these the New Theology still teaches that Christ came to this earth with the nature of Adam before the fall. They do this primarily to avoid the truth that Christ is our example and that we are called to live a sinless life as He did. The New Theology, similar to what most of Christianity is doing today, is simply lowering the standard. Sadly, those who are doing this are only deceiving themselves and forfeiting all that God offers to them, just to *enjoy the pleasures of sin for a season.*

The other reason I wanted to examine some of the views, as well as lifestyles, of those on the liberal side is because I hope that by doing so I can make one very important point. If you see the validity of this point—and I am convinced that it cannot be missed and it cannot be denied—hopefully it will make you more aware of the necessity of finding out whether I am right or not in regard to my assertion that many conservative Seventh-day Adventists have accepted 'another Jesus.'

I think it can be truthfully said, that in most cases the real reason why people embrace the 'theology' of the New Theology is because it allows them to accept a lower standard, which in turn allows them to be more worldly and self-indulgent. In my mind, both the theology and the lifestyle of those who believe in the New Theology are so obviously different from true Bible religion and true righteousness that it cannot possibly even begin to meet the description given in these two quotes that I am about to share. And if not, that would mean that we must look elsewhere for the fulfillment of these warnings:

> "So well will [Satan] counterfeit righteousness, that if it were possible, he would deceive the very elect."
> { *Fundamentals of Christian Education* 472 }

> "So closely will the counterfeit resemble the true that it will be impossible to distinguish between them except by the Holy Scriptures. By their testimony every statement and every miracle must be tested." { *Great Controversy* 593 }

Chapter 8

"REDEMPTION IS THAT PROCESS..."

It is a truth that is beyond human comprehension; it is a truth that should fill our hearts with undying love and gratitude; and it is a truth that should make the world and everything it has to offer seem as nothing: that every single one of us, though fallen and degraded through sin, can, through the power of God and our own diligent effort, actually and truly become like Christ:

> "*All* who study the life of Christ and practice His teachings will become like Christ." {*Evangelism* 269}

There are other important truths that need to be correctly understood and properly combined with this great truth, especially as it relates to having a correct understanding of the life of Christ.

The first truth I want to point out, a truth that in some ways does not even need to be pointed out, yet for the purpose of leading us to another truth, does need to be pointed out, is brought to view in the last few words of that quote from Evangelism: '...*will become* like Christ.' It is a truth that every true child of God has often been made painfully aware of: that as wonderful a miracle that it is to come *to Christ*, there is still much changing to be done before we become fully *like Christ*:

> "Man has fallen; and it will be the work of a lifetime, be it longer or shorter, to recover from that fall, and regain, through Christ, the image of the divine."
>
> {*2 Testimonies* 448}

> "Redemption is that process by which the soul is trained for heaven. This training means a knowledge of Christ. It means emancipation from ideas, habits, and practices that

have been gained in the school of the prince of darkness."
{*Desire of Ages* 330}

Another truth that I want to point out, right along side of that last one, is that some have descended much deeper into the 'pit of sin' than others, and therefore have a great deal more ideas, habits, and practices that they need to be emancipated from:

"The souls who came to Jesus felt in His presence that even for them there was escape from the pit of sin...Their very misery and sin made them only the more the objects of His compassion. The farther they had wandered from Him, the more earnest the longing and the greater the sacrifice for their rescue."   {*Christ's Object Lessons* 186}

"The chain that is let down from the throne of God is long enough to reach into the lowest depths of sin...He is able to reach to the lowest depths and lift them up from the pit of sin, that they may be acknowledged as children of God, heirs with Christ to an immortal inheritance. They may have the life that measures with the life of God."
{*Review & Herald*, Nov. 26, 1895}

"He passed by no human being as worthless, but sought to apply the saving remedy to every soul. In whatever company He found Himself, He presented a lesson that was appropriate to the time and the circumstances. He sought to inspire with hope the most rough and unpromising, setting before them the assurance that they might become blameless and harmless, attaining such a character as would make them manifest as the children of God. Often He met those who had drifted under Satan's control, and who had no power to break from his snare. To such a one, discouraged, sick, tempted, and fallen, Jesus would speak words of tenderest pity, words that were needed and could be understood."   {*Desire of Ages* 91}

(I often wish that every human being could just read the Spirit of Prophecy.)

I would like to combine one more truth with those other truths.

It has always been true, and it always will be true, that:

"The Scriptures are the great agency in the transformation of character." {*Christ's Object Lessons* 100}

Every step of the way, from the lowest depths to the very heights of glory, God, through His word, guides us, warns us, encourages us, strengthens us, corrects us, and transforms us. (His word is certainly not the only agency through which He works, but it is the one through which all others are to be tested.)

Now I want to try to put all of this together in a way that will help to keep us from falling into that trap the Spirit of Prophecy warns us about:

"Let every human being be warned from the ground of making Christ altogether human, such an one as ourselves; for it cannot be." {*5 Bible Commentary* 1129}

Many of the quotes that I have used in this chapter make it abundantly clear that there are tremendous changes that need to take place in order to transform a fallen human being into the likeness of Christ. And as the next quote will so solemnly explain, these changes are not instantaneous (neither do they come easily). And right here is where I want to stress what to me is a very important point: God, in His infinite wisdom and love, has given us instruction and help for every step of the way. Words that are given to help me to overcome a particular problem at a certain stage of my growth may not be at all necessary for you; and visa versa. We have to be very careful not to take certain truths that are specifically designed to meet us in our less than perfect conditions and improperly apply them to Christ.

Now that solemn quote I mentioned up above:

"The infinite value of the sacrifice required for our redemption reveals the fact that sin is a tremendous evil...

"Wrongs cannot be righted, nor can reformations in conduct be made by a few feeble, intermittent efforts. Character building is the work, not of a day, nor of a year, but of a lifetime. The struggle for conquest over self, for holiness and heaven, is a lifelong struggle. Without continual effort and constant activity, there can be no advancement in the divine life, no attainment of the victor's crown.

"The strongest evidence of man's fall from a higher state is the fact that it costs so much to return. The way of return can be gained only by hard fighting, inch by inch, hour by hour. In one moment, by a hasty, unguarded act, we may place ourselves in the power of evil; but it requires more than a moment to break the fetters and attain to a holier life. The purpose may be formed, the work begun; but its accomplishment will require toil, time, perseverance, patience, and sacrifice." {*Ministry of Healing* 451, 452}

I would like to say one thing in reference to that last quote before continuing on. Please be extremely careful about accepting any message that would lessen the force of those words. Any message that promises holiness apart from the path marked out in that quote is certain to lead to one of two places: utter discouragement or a false experience.

I have never been very good or very open in giving my 'testimony'; but as I sit here reading over some of those earlier quotes I feel as if my heart is breaking and must express itself; hopefully to the glory of God and to the encouraging and uplifting of others who have fallen into the pit of sin.

I spent the first twenty-some years of my life *"without Christ...and without God in the world"* {Ephesians 2:12}, and managed to 'gain' some very destructive 'habits and practices in the school of the prince of darkness'. I found out many years ago that 'it costs so much to return.' I believe with all my heart that the Spirit of Prophecy, as always, is right when it says: 'The way of return can be gained only by hard fighting, inch by inch, hour by hour.' I have also found out all too many times, and all too painfully, that she is also right, when she says: '...by a hasty, unguarded act, we may place ourselves in the power of evil'. But I can also tell you that I have found the *'pearl of great price'*, and that the years of pain and struggle are as nothing compared to it. (This is not to say that the pain and struggles are all over. But I can honestly tell you that the way continually gets better and brighter. I can also honestly tell you that I would not trade where I am at right now for anything in the world.) And to every one of you, no matter where you have been, or where you are at now, I say with Jeremiah, *"Seek Him with all your heart and you will find Him."* {Jer. 29:13} I say with Paul, *'Everything else is worthless when compared to knowing Him.'* {Phil. 3:8 NLT} And I say with Ellen White:

> *"Not one* who complies with the conditions will be disappointed at the end of the race. *Not one* who is earnest and persevering will fail of success. The race is not to the swift, or the battle to the strong. The weakest saint, as well as the strongest, may wear the crown of immortal glory. *All* may win who, through the power of divine grace, bring their lives into conformity to the will of Christ."
>
> {*Acts of the Apostles* 313}

Chapter 9

"TEMPTATION IS..."

I hope that every chapter I have written is important and necessary. At the same time, when it comes to understanding the experience of Christ in relation to His being tempted, and what that means to us personally, this chapter is crucial.

Over many years of talking and studying with people my wife and I have come to realize that there is a very common, yet very serious, misunderstanding of what it means to be 'tempted.' Closely connected with this misunderstanding is a failure to realize that as with so many other subjects and words in the Bible the word tempted can have more than one meaning.

The primary meaning of the word temptation is clearly given in this quote:

> "Temptation is enticement to sin, and this does not proceed from God, but from Satan and from the evil of our own hearts."   {*Mount of Blessing* 116}

Satan tried everything he possibly could to 'entice' Jesus to sin. (As we read earlier: 'Satan left no means untried to ensnare Jesus.') Ellen White, in that quote from *Mount of Blessing* tells us that: 'temptation is enticement to sin.' And it is in this sense that it can truly be said of Christ, 'He was in all points tempted like as we are.'

Right here is where a critical distinction needs to be made and understood: while 'temptation is enticement to sin', how that enticement is perceived and received by us, and how we react to that enticement is an entirely separate matter. Multitudes of Seventh-day Adventists, conservatives and liberals alike, laymen and ministers alike, hold the mistaken understanding that temptation is only temptation if in some way we find it desirable; that temptation is only temptation if we find it 'tempting'. I cannot overemphasize the importance of coming to a correct understanding of this.

Let me begin with an example that I believe is so clear that no one can fail to see that to apply the above understanding of temptation to this would be ludicrous. And because of the nature of the quote let me try to explain something before beginning.

This study began, and basically centers on the verse:

> "Every man is tempted when he is drawn away of his own lust." {James 1:14}

In the next chapter I will be spending more time on the meaning of the word lust in this verse, but right now, because of the nature of this upcoming quote, I want to look at the words 'man', 'he', and 'his' in this verse. I do not believe that the Bible writer, in this case James, intended to limit this verse strictly to men. The King James often uses the term 'man' or 'men' when really wanting to express the idea of mankind or human beings. Every one of the others translations that I have apply this verse to all people. I hope to make it even clearer in the next chapter that James is really intending to say: 'Every human being is tempted...'

I bring this out here because this next quote, instead of dealing with men being tempted by women, deals with women being tempted by men. (Because it is such important and timely counsel I will include the entire paragraph.):

> "The slightest insinuations, from whatever source they may come, inviting you to indulge in sin or to allow the least unwarrantable liberty with your persons, should be resented as the worst of insults to your dignified woman-hood. The kiss upon your cheek, at an improper time and place, should lead you to repel the emissary of Satan with disgust. If it is from one in high places who is dealing in sacred things, the sin is of tenfold greater magnitude, and should lead a God-fearing woman or youth to recoil with horror, not only from the sin he would have you commit, but from the hypocrisy and villainy of one whom the people

respect and honor as God's servant. He is handling sacred things, yet hiding his baseness of heart under a ministerial cloak. Be afraid of anything like this familiarity. Be sure that the least approach to it is evidence of a lascivious mind and a lustful eye. If the least encouragement is given in this direction, if any of the liberties mentioned are tolerated, no better evidence can be given that your mind is not pure and chaste as it should be, and that sin and crime have charms for you. You lower the standard of your dignified, virtuous womanhood, and give unmistakable evidence that a low, brutal, common passion and lust has been suffered to remain alive in your heart and has never been crucified."

{*2 Testimonies* 458, 459}

The first sentence in that quote says: 'The slightest insinuations...*inviting you to indulge in sin*...' Clearly, this is 'enticement to sin', which Ellen White tells us is 'temptation'. It is just as clear, that in the mind of Ellen White, a godly woman would find this anything but desirable, anything but tempting. As a matter of fact, she uses words that would describe a response completely the opposite of desirable: *'disgust'* and *'recoil with horror'*. There is no way in all the world that anyone could possibly get the understanding from this quote that when 'a God-fearing woman' encounters this temptation, she is being, 'drawn away of [her] own lust.'

Before leaving this quote I would like to ask you to carefully re-read the last two sentences of it and to take note of the context in which Ellen White places lust.

Now I would like to look at two quotes concerning Christ that will shed wonderful light on this question of what it means to be tempted. These two quotes are so perfectly designed to help us understand this point that one could easily believe that God ordained them specifically for this reason.

The first quote is Ellen White's interpretation of the verse: "For in that he himself hath suffered being tempted, he is able to succour them that are tempted." {Hebrews 2:18} Her first words are:

"Would that we could comprehend the significance of the words, Christ 'suffered being tempted.'"

{*7 Bible Commentary* 927}
{*Review & Herald*, November 8, 1887}

Is not this exactly what we need to help us answer our question? And is not Ellen White going to go on to tell us exactly how we should comprehend the words, 'Christ suffered being tempted?'

"Would that we could comprehend the significance of the words, Christ 'suffered being tempted.' While He was free from the taint of sin, the refined sensibilities of His holy nature rendered contact with evil unspeakably painful to Him." {*7 Bible Commentary* 927}
{*Review & Herald*, November 8, 1887}

Ellen White is explaining to us that the words, 'Christ suffered being tempted,' are to be understood—not in the sense that He desired to indulge in the sin that He was being tempted with—but that the refined sensibilities of His holy nature rendered contact with this temptation unspeakably painful to Him. This is the exact same picture as presented with the Godly woman that was invited to indulge in sin: she finds it 'disgusting' and 'recoils with horror'; Christ finds it 'unspeakably painful'.

Let me try to make this unmistakably clear by using an illustration. And since this whole question (up to this point) pivots on peoples understanding of the text—'every man is tempted when he is drawn away of his own lust'—allow me to illustrate this in the context of immorality and lust: How would a godly father and mother feel if their beloved daughter turned to all kinds of immoral behavior, even going so far as to become a harlot or a prostitute? Would it not be 'unspeakably painful' to them? Now try to realize how horrible the suffering must have been, when Christ 'suffered being tempted', by not only having to see these young women behaving themselves in this manner, but even having some of them (those who were so fully under the control of Satan that they allowed themselves to be used of him in his efforts to overcome Christ) entice Him and try to lure Him into sin. Try to realize that every single one of these young women were His own children by creation. Try to realize that He was about to die for them. Try to realize that He loved these women with a love that is infinitely greater than the love of any earthly father or mother for their daughter. And try to realize, as we read earlier, that He was 'Infinite Purity.' To see these young women, His own beloved children, being used of Satan in such a disgusting and degrading manner must have caused Him a degree of pain and sorrow that we can hardly begin to comprehend. Who in their right mind can possibly believe that all the while Christ was experiencing those kind of thoughts and feelings, He was at the same time being 'drawn away of His own lust.'

The second quote I want to look at is Ellen White's insight into exactly what Christ was thinking and experiencing during the third temptation in the wilderness. This is the temptation where Satan showed Christ all the kingdoms of the world and tried to get Christ to worship him. Once again, her first words show how perfectly suited this quote is to help answer our question of what it means to be tempted:

> "This was to Christ just what the Bible declares it to be—a temptation." {*5 Bible Commentary* 1083}

As you read through the remainder of the quote pay particularly close attention to Ellen White's description of what Christ actually saw while Satan was presenting to Him this temptation:

> "This was to Christ just what the Bible declares it to be—a temptation. Before His sight the tempter held the kingdoms of the world. As Satan saw them, they possessed great external grandeur. But Christ saw them in a different aspect, just as they were—earthly dominions under the power of a tyrant. He saw humanity full of woe, suffering under the oppressive power of Satan. He saw the earth defiled by hatred, revenge, malice, lust, and murder. He saw fiends in the possession of the bodies and souls of men."
> {*5 Bible Commentary* 1083}

If you saw 'earthly dominions under the power of a tyrant'; if you saw 'humanity full of woe, suffering under the oppressive power of Satan'; if you saw 'the earth defiled by hatred, revenge, malice, lust, and murder'; and if you saw 'fiends in the possession of the bodies and souls of men;' would you find those things 'tempting'; would you find yourself 'being drawn away of your own lust' to have them? I think not!

Yet still Ellen White tells us:

> "This was to Christ just what the Bible declares it to be—a temptation."   {5 *Bible Commentaries* 1083}

This is a perfect example of temptation: both from the view of the 'tempter' and the 'tempted'; and much can be learned from it. In this case the tempter was Satan himself, but in most cases the tempter is some human agent through whom he is able to work. The tempter tries to make his temptation appear as attractive and desirable as possible, and all too often that is exactly how the tempted sees it, which is a major factor in why the person yields to the temptation. But—and this is a most crucial and wonderful truth—if the person being tempted is one with his Heavenly Father, as Jesus was; and if he is full of the Holy Spirit, as Jesus was; and if he is 'dead indeed unto sin', as Paul tells him to be, and as Jesus was; and if he loves his Heavenly Father with all his heart and soul and mind, as Jesus did; then, instead of the temptation appearing beautiful and attractive, as the tempter is trying to make it appear; the tempted will 'see it in a different aspect, just as it is'; then, as Ellen White tells us, the tempted will hate it as the vile thing it is:

> "O that we may cultivate habits of contemplation of the self-denial and self-sacrifice of the life of Christ, until we shall have a deep sense of the aggravating character of sin, and hate it as the vile thing it is."   {*I Selected Messages* 106}

> "We...should...abhor sin as the hateful thing it is."
>   {*Our High Calling* 94}

"Appetite and passion are overcoming thousands of Christ's professed followers. Their senses become so blunted on account of familiarity with sin that they do not abhor it, but view it as attractive." {*3 Testimonies* 473}

Now, as for the word 'tempted' having more than one usage, or meaning. First of all, the Spirit of Prophecy informs us:

"There is a difference between being tempted, and entering into temptation." {*Temperance* 192}

And we saw earlier how she explained James 1:14:

"Says the apostle, "Every man is tempted [that is, enters into temptation] when he is drawn away of his own lust and enticed." {*Signs of the Times*, March 9, 1882}

Putting these two quotes together, it should be easy to see that James 1:14 cannot be the description of a person 'being tempted', because the *Signs of the Times* quote clearly tells us it is the description of a person 'entering into temptation', and the *Temperance* quote clearly tells us 'there is a difference between being temped, and entering into temptation.'

So we see from this that when we encounter the word tempted in the Bible we need to ask ourselves: is the Bible writer using the word tempted in the sense of 'being tempted', or is he using it in the sense of 'entering into temptation.'

Now let me examine two other verses where the word tempted is being used in the sense of 'entering into temptation.' Galatians 6:1 is one of them:

"Brethren, if a man be overtaken in a fault, ye which are spiritual, restore such an one in the spirit of meekness; considering thyself, *lest thou also be tempted*." {Galatians 6:1}

Paul's meaning of the word tempted in this verse, like James 1:14, must be 'entering into temptation' rather than 'being tempted', for Paul most certainly understood the truth that, *"all are exposed to temptation."* {*DA* 414}

When we combine all that we've just learned about the usage and meaning of the word tempted, Paul's warning in Galatians 6:1 is seen to be just another way of repeating Christ's warning in Mark 14:38:

> "...considering thyself, lest thou also be tempted"
>
> {Galatians 6:1}

> "Watch ye and pray, lest ye enter into temptation."
>
> {Mark 14:38}

First Thessalonians chapter three is another example. Paul was so worried that the Thessalonians had fallen into sin that he finally sent Timothy to find out:

> "For this cause, when I could no longer forbear, I sent [Timotheus] to know your faith, lest by some means the tempter have tempted you, and our labor be in vain."
>
> {1 Thessalonians 3:2, 5}

I think this is an excellent opportunity to demonstrate the benefit of using multiple translations; at the same time this would probably be a good opportunity to briefly examine the belief that the King James is the only translation that is safe to use.

There are a number of Bibles that I use occasionally, but there are two that I use all the time: the King James and the New Living. Ninety-five percent of the time the two translations are basically saying the same thing, only in different words. (That is pretty much the way it is with all translations.) But I must tell you, I have found that in many instances the New Living translates a passage, not in a way that contradicts the King James, but in a way that expresses more clearly to our minds exactly what it is that the Bible writer was intending to convey. Paul's use of the word tempted in those two verses from Galatians and First Thessalonians is a perfect example:

> "Dear brothers and sisters, if another Christian is overcome by some sin, you who are godly should gently and

humbly help that person back onto the right path. *And be careful not to fall into the same temptation yourself.*"

{Galatians 6:1 NLT}

"That is why, when I could bear it no longer, I sent Timothy to find out whether your faith was still strong. *I was afraid that the Tempter had gotten the best of you...*"

{I Thessalonians 3:5 NLT}

Even as I sit here examining and writing about these verses it continues to grow clearer that both translations are saying the same thing, only the New Living grasps and expresses the meaning better. Take Galatians 6:1 for example: the King James starts out with the words: 'Brethren, if a man be overtaken...', and ends with the words: 'lest thou also be tempted.' The words 'thou also' can only be referring back to the man who was 'overtaken'. Paul was clearly saying: 'lest thou also be overtaken.' The translators of the New Living realized that, and therefore translated the last portion of the verse in a way that clearly expresses that.

The same is true in the First Thessalonians passage. In verse one and verse five of First Thessalonians chapter three we read that Paul was so worried about the Thessalonians that he 'could no longer forbear.' All of the modern translations I have translate that portion more along the lines of: 'when I could no longer stand it', or, 'when I could no longer bear it', which is exactly what the King James is saying. What is it that Paul could no longer bear? It certainly wasn't the fact that they might be exposed to 'being tempted.' Paul knew all too well that they were 'being tempted' (just read verses 3 & 4). It had to be that they might have 'entered into temptation.' And that is why in place of the King James saying: 'lest by some means the tempter have tempted you', the New Living says: 'I was afraid that the Tempter had gotten the best of you.' And that is also why Paul finishes with the words: 'and our labor be in vain.'

Now I would like to take a brief look at the teaching that the King James is the only Bible that should be used. The first argument I would make, the argument that I feel should settle the whole question, is the fact that Ellen White often quoted from the Revised Version, as well as occasionally from other translations. Why do you think she did that? Do you think that she just randomly decided to quote from a different translation? Of course not! Obviously she felt that the other Bible translated some aspect of that particular verse in a way that expressed the truth that God wanted us to know in a better, or clearer, or more powerful way. Along with that comes one of two unavoidable conclusions: #1—Ellen White must have been fairly familiar with those different translations, otherwise how would she have had any idea when to substitute them for the King James; or, #2—she went looking through those other translations to see if they stated the verse in a way that was clearer or better. Either way, if God's inspired prophet, who we know was led of the Spirit, made use of other translations, so should we. (Slowly flip through *8 Testimonies* 262-285 and you will be convinced.)

Daniel 7:9 is a classic example, as well as an extremely important one for Seventh-day Adventists, of an instance where the modern translations undeniably translate the verse in a way that makes it much easier for the reader to come to a correct understanding of what the Bible writer was actually wanting to say. The King James reads:

"I beheld till the thrones *were cast down*"

All modern translations I have ever seen read more like this:

"I kept looking until thrones *were set up*"   {NASB}

or

"I watched as thrones *were put in place*"   {NLT}

Ellen White, in both the 1888 and 1911 editions of *The Great Controversy* quotes Daniel 7:9 from the Revised Version:

"I beheld till thrones *were placed*"

Stephen Haskell in his book, *The Story of Daniel the Prophet* uses two different translations. And Uriah Smith in his classic, *Daniel and the Revelation* says:

"By an unfortunate translation in verse 9, a wrong idea is almost sure to be conveyed. The words *cast down* are from a word which in the original signifies just the opposite, namely, to set up."

{*Daniel and the Revelation*; his comment on Daniel 7:9}

Since I mentioned the 1888 and 1911 editions of *The Great Controversy*, I would like to touch briefly on a similar teaching that some of you have probably encountered: that the original edition of *The Great Controversy*, which is the 1884 edition, also known as *Spirit of Prophecy Volume IV*, is the only edition of *The Great Controversy* that is safe to read. The proponents of this teaching say that the church has so tampered with The Great Controversy that it is no longer giving the message that Ellen White intended it to give. I believe this is nothing but a distraction from the devil and another manifestation of the fulfillment of the warning:

"The very last deception of Satan will be to make of none effect the testimony of the Spirit of God...Satan will work ingeniously, in different ways and through different agencies, to unsettle the confidence of God's remnant people in the true testimony."   {*I Selected Messages* 48}

This next quote is a statement by Ellen White herself concerning the 1911 edition of *The Great Controversy*. It is found in the supplement of *Spirit of Prophecy Vol. IV*. (I will quote it exactly as it is in the supplement):

"A few days ago I received a copy of the new edition of the book Great Controversy, recently printed at Washington. The book pleases me. I have spent many hours looking through its pages, and I see that the publishing houses have done good work...

"Recently it was necessary for this book to be reset, because the electrotype plates were badly worn. It has cost me much to have this done, but I don't complain; for whatever the cost may be, I regard this new edition with great satisfaction...

"When I learned that Great Controversy must be reset, I determined that we would have everything closely examined, to see if the truths it contained were stated in the very best manner, to convince those not of our faith that the Lord had guided and sustained me in the writing of its pages.

"As a result of the thorough examination by our most experienced workers, some changing in the wording has been proposed. These changes I have carefully examined, and approved. I am thankful my life has been spared, and that I have strength and clearness of mind for this and other literary work."

—Letter 56, 1911 {*Spirit of Prophecy Volume IV* 530}

In the desire to not leave a wrong impression, I need to try to make one thing clear before going on to the next chapter. In chapter eight I spent a good deal of time looking at the fact that redemption is a process; that we do not go from a lifetime of wrong habits and practices to Christ-like perfection overnight. There may often be times, especially in the earlier stages of our Christian life, when there is a part of us that does 'desire' to commit the sin that Satan is trying to entice us with. The thing I want to try to make clear is: I believe that a victory is definitely gained if we do not give in to those desires. But (and here is the part that I believe is so critical), this was never the experience of Jesus; and equally important, as we 'grow up to the full stature of men and women in Christ' we must, and will, come more and more to the point where these temptations have no appeal to us whatsoever, and we actually come to hate them:

"Those who become new creatures in Christ Jesus...will no longer fashion themselves according to the former lusts, but by the faith of the Son of God they will follow in His steps, reflect His character, and purify themselves even as He is pure. The things they once hated they now love, and the things they once loved they hate." {*Steps to Christ* 58}

"TEMPTATION IS..."

"When the sinner has a view of the matchless charms of Jesus, sin no longer looks attractive to him; for he beholds the Chiefest among ten thousand, the One altogether lovely." {*Faith and Works* 107}

Chapter 10

"...IT HAS A BROADER MEANING"

Keeping in mind what we just studied in chapter nine concerning the mistaken understanding that in order for something to be a temptation we have to desire it, I would like to return to something I said earlier. In chapter five I stated that this whole subject of lust, temptation, and James 1:14 covers a much broader realm than just sexual things. In the Bible itself the word lust is actually used as often in a non-sexual connotation as it is in a sexual. Here are just a few examples:

> "The enemy said, I will pursue, I will overtake, I will divide the spoil; my lust shall be satisfied upon them; I will draw my sword, my hand shall destroy them."
> {Exodus 15:9}

> "They [asked] meat for their lust."   {Psalms 78:18}

> "From whence come wars and fightings among you? come they not hence, even of your lusts..."   {James 4:1}

Ellen White makes a comment on I Peter 2:11 ("Abstain from fleshly lusts, which war against the soul."), that I believe can also be said of James 1:14:

> "Many regard this text as a warning against licentiousness only; *but it has a broader meaning*".
> {*Counsel of Diet and Foods* 167}

Often in the Bible the word lust is used in the much broader sense of 'evil desire'; which is exactly how most modern Bibles translate James 1:14:

"It is the evil that a person wants that tempts him. His own evil desire leads him away and holds him."
{International Children's Version}

"Each one is tempted when, by his own evil desire, he is dragged away..."   {New International Version}

"Temptation comes from the lure of our own evil desires."   {New Living Bible}

"It is the evil that a person wants that tempts him. His own evil desires lead him away and hold him."
{Billy Graham Translation}

I believe it is no coincidence that almost all Bibles translate the word 'lust' here exactly the same: 'evil desires'. It must also be kept in mind that in every translation, including the King James, are found the words: 'his own' or 'our own'. And it is right here that this whole subject not only centers, but where it also embraces virtually every aspect of life. I only hope that I can express what is being taught in a way that will cause people to realize that something is seriously wrong.

Before saying what I am going to say here, let me also remind you that what I am about to describe is not the understanding and experience of those who have embraced the beliefs of the New Theology (although I cannot help but imagine that there are some who have turned to the New Theology because they never found true peace and true victory in the belief and experience that I am about to describe). What I am about to describe is the understanding and experience of multitudes of fundamental, conservative, old-fashioned Seventh-day Adventists, who truly love the great truths that have been committed to us as the remnant people. And this stretches from the most insignificant layman to the highest theologians and preachers.

Here is what is believed and taught (and I must say, it would be virtually impossible for a man to teach this if this were not his own experience): There was always a part of Christ that wanted to do wrong. (This is usually attributed to the fact that Christ, like all human beings, had a fallen nature. I will be sharing some quotes in chapter twelve that will shed light on this question of our fallen nature.) Again, here is what is being taught: There was always a part of Christ that wanted to do wrong: He was 'drawn away of His own evil desires' (sometimes stated as 'evil tendencies'), but He never gave in to them. Of course it must then be taught that there will always be a part of us that wants to do wrong: we will always be 'drawn away of our own evil desires'; but as long as we never give in to them, this is not only victory, but Christian perfection.

Let me stop here and repeat what I tried to make clear in the last chapter: Since Christianity involves a process ('redemption is that process' *DA* 330) of growing up into the full stature of men and women in Christ Jesus, there may very well be times when saying no to 'our own evil desires' will truly be victory. But this is not the ultimate experience that God is calling us to, it most certainly was never the experience of Christ, and, possibly what is of greatest importance right now, it is not the kind of experience that will ever bring about the fulfillment of these words:

> "When the character of Christ shall be perfectly repro-
> duced in His people, then He will come to claim them as
> His own."   {*Christ's Object Lessons* 69}

I would like to spend the rest of this chapter looking at a number of quotes, and then commenting on them in an attempt to show how out of harmony this teaching is with the Spirit of Prophecy. (I will also be including one quote from an additional author.) There can be no denying that these quotes are not only wonderful, but that all of us need, more than anything else in the world, to have them written in our hearts and minds. It is this, and only this, that will forever settle this whole question.

I want to share one all-important quote before beginning:

> "[The reception of truth] depends upon the renunciation
> of every sin that the Spirit of God reveals."
>
> {*Desire of Ages* 455}

Please, before going on: STOP; and if you have never truly done it before, commit yourself to God with a commitment that holds back absolutely nothing. Determine in your heart that you will follow Christ and His truth no matter what it costs you. That you will give up every single thought and practice that is not in perfect harmony with the revealed will of God, no matter how small or how dear it may seem to you.

I would like to begin with a most important Bible text; it has to do with hating sin (as well as loving righteousness); then I will share some quotes that will go along with it:

> "But unto the Son he saith...Thou hast loved righteous-
> ness, and hated iniquity; therefore ..."   {Hebrews 1:8, 9}

Since this next quote is from someone other than Ellen White, I feel that I must preface it with the Bible admonition: *'Prove all things; hold fast that which is good.'* Having said that, I would now like to say a little bit about the man before citing his words. The man is Charles Fitch. He, along with William Miller and many others, preached the great Second Advent message throughout the early 1840's. In vision Ellen White saw him in heaven:

> "Here we saw the tree of life and the throne of God...We
> all went under the tree and sat down to look at the glory of
> the place, when Brethren Fitch and Stockman, who had
> preached the gospel of the kingdom, and whom God had
> laid in the grave to save them, came up to us and asked us
> what we had passed through while they were sleeping."
> {*Early Writings* 17}

I have heard it said that Charles Fitch was the most beloved advent preacher. After reading his writings I can certainly understand why. Here is what he had to say in regard to loving righteousness and hating iniquity:

> "The all-absorbing question with me then, so far as my
> own eternal interests are concerned, is this: How shall I
> become obedient to that high command of the most high

God, "Be ye holy for I am holy!" (I Peter 1:16; Leviticus 11:44). I have, I can have, I ought to have, no expectation of dwelling where God dwells—of being an object of His love forever, and a sharer of the eternal blessedness which He only can give, unless I have a character fully assimilated to His—unless I love, with a full and undivided heart, what He loves, and hate what He hates, and all that He hates, with a hatred, full, entire, uniform, perpetual, like His own."

{ *Sin Shall Not Have Dominion Over You* 4, 5 }

Allow me to use this opportunity to try to convince you to obtain a copy of his book. My wife and I, along with scores of others, would honestly tell you that outside of the Bible and the Spirit of Prophecy it is the most powerful and beautiful book we have ever read. It is all about living a sinless life. He uses the Bible in a way that is absolutely wonderful. It is clear that for him righteousness and holiness were not just a theory, but his actual experience. I believe it is this that gives his book such power. (And it was this that gave the Second Advent movement such power. And it is this, and only this, that will give us the power that we so desperately need to finish the work.) Since there are no Spirit of Prophecy quotes in it, it is an absolutely wonderful missionary book. If you are not able to find it at the ABC's, or through one of the independent book sellers, you can obtain a copy from my wife and me. Providentially we had a part in the initial publishing of it (thanks to a dear friend who searched high and low for these kinds of old writings). If you decide you want one there is contact information in the back of the book.

Now some quotes from the Spirit of Prophecy about hating sin:

"There is only one power that can guide the heart and mind in paths of truth and righteousness. We must know the love of Christ in our individual experience. This love in the soul will purify the entire being and renew it in the likeness of God. More and more familiar are we to become with Christ's divine human life; we are to make it ours by personal experience, until it can be said of us as it was said of

Him, "Thou hast loved righteousness, and hated iniquity."
{*Signs of the Times*, January 20, 1909}

What a quote!

Ask yourself the question: when 'our individual experience' is the experience described in those words: 'this love in the soul will purify the entire being and renew it [the entire being] in the likeness of God', what part of our being will still want to do wrong?

This next quote has long been one of my favorites:

"All true obedience comes from the heart. It was heart work with Christ. And if we consent, He will so identify Himself with our thoughts and aims, so blend our hearts and minds into conformity to His will, that when obeying Him we shall be but carrying out our own impulses. The will, refined and sanctified, will find its highest delight in doing His service. When we know God as it is our privilege to know Him, our life will be a life of continual obedience. Through an appreciation of the character of Christ, through communion with God, sin will become hateful to us." {*Desire of Ages* 668}

Please, read that quote over and over and over. Can a person truly have this kind of experience and at the same time want to do wrong?

Earlier I used the quote:

"Never before had there been a being upon the earth who *hated sin with so perfect a hatred* as did Christ." {*I Selected Messages* 254}

Now I want to share a quote that shows we can hate sin with a perfect hatred also (this is not the only quote of its kind):

"O, if every one could see this matter as it is presented before me in all its bearings, how soon would they quit with the enemy in his artful work! How they would despise his measures to bring sin upon the human family! How they would *hate sin with a perfect hatred*, as they consider the fact that it cost the life of heaven's Commander, in order that they should not perish, that man should not be bound a hopeless captive to Satan's chariot, a degraded slave to his will, a trophy of his victory and his kingdom."

{*Fundamentals of Christian Education* 291}

As I said earlier, I cannot fathom how someone could want to do something they have a perfect hatred for.

Now I would like to spend a few minutes considering this question from a different perspective: I have repeatedly stressed the truth that we are called to become like Christ. Do you realize that we are also called to become like God?

"Higher than the highest human thought can reach is God's ideal for His children. Godliness—godlikeness—is the goal to be reached."　　　　{*Education* 18}

"The righteousness of God is absolute. This righteousness characterizes all His works, all His laws. As God is, so must His people be."　　　　{*I Selected Messages* 198}

All of us are probably familiar with Christ's command at the end of His Sermon on the Mount:

"Be ye therefore perfect, even as your Father which is in heaven is perfect."　　　　{Matthew 5:48}

Commenting on this verse, Ellen White tells us:

"The conditions of eternal life, under grace, are just what they were in Eden—perfect righteousness, harmony with God…God has made provision that we may become like unto Him…He tells us to be perfect as He is, in the same manner…Jesus said, Be perfect as your Father is perfect…"

{*Mount of Blessing* 76, 77}

I began this point by saying: "I have repeatedly stressed the truth that we are called to become like Christ. Do you realize that we are also called to become like God?" Do I believe that becoming like Christ and becoming like God are one in the same thing? I answer unequivocally—yes:

> "He that hath seen Me hath seen the Father."
> {John 14:9}

> "I and my Father are one."   {John 10:30}

To avoid the possibility of any misunderstanding: I <u>DO NOT</u> believe that God the Father and Christ (who, in the truest sense was, and is, also God) are the same person. They are two separate and distinct individuals:

> "The unity that exists between Christ and His disciples does not destroy the personality of either. They are one in purpose, in mind, in character, but not in person. It is thus that God and Christ are one." {*Ministry of Healing* 422}

Ellen White, commenting on those two verses from John says:

> "The glory of the Father was revealed in the Son; Christ made manifest the character of the Father. He was so perfectly connected with God, so completely embraced in His encircling light, that he who had seen the Son, had seen the Father." {*Review & Herald,* January 7, 1890}
> {*5 Bible Commentary* 1142}

"As a personal being, God has revealed Himself in His Son...Christ, the Light of the world, veiled the dazzling splendor of His divinity and came to live as a man among men, that they might, without being consumed, become acquainted with their Creator. Since sin brought separation between man and his Maker, no man has seen God at any time, except as He is manifested through Christ...

"God saw that a clearer revelation than nature was needed to portray both His personality and His character. He sent His Son into the world to manifest, so far as could

be endured by human sight, the nature and the attributes of
the invisible God."   {*Ministry of Healing* 418, 419}

Jesus made one of the most important statements in the
history of the world when He declared: 'He that has seen Me
hath seen the Father.' To paint the picture that outwardly Christ
was 'manifesting the nature and the attributes of the invisible
God', while inwardly He was being 'drawn away of His own lust',
or being 'drawn away of His own evil desires', is, to put it in the
words of inspiration, truly error:

"...of a most startling nature."   {*I Selected Messages* 197}

"...misrepresents [Christ] and is a dishonor to His greatness and majesty."   {*8 Testimonies* 291}

and has

"...sensuality [as its] sphere."   {*8 Testimonies* 291}

(Those last three quotes are all related. I will leave it to you to
find out how.)

Chapter 11

"NOT MY WILL, BUT THINE"

These words of Christ are, unfortunately, often used to lend support to this belief that there was a part of Him that wanted to do wrong. Hopefully by taking a closer look at them it will be seen that nothing could be further from the truth.

There were actually three different occasions in which Christ made this kind of statement: John 5:30, John 6:38, and Gethsemane. The statements in John 5:30 and 6:38 are similar and I will look at them as one. Those words spoken in Gethsemane were undeniably of a completely different nature than the ones in John 5 and 6. I will look at the statements in John 5 and 6 first, then I will examine Christ's words in Gethsemane.

Here are the two statements from John 5 and 6:

> "I seek not mine own will, but the will of the Father which hath sent me."   {John 5:30}

> "I came down from heaven, not to do mine own will, but the will of him that sent me."   {John 6:38}

I hope that two quotes will be sufficient to show what a horrible misapplication it is to use those words of Christ in John 5 and 6 to support the idea that Christ's will was different from His Father's, or that there was a part of Him that wanted to do wrong:

> "The time of the Passover was drawing near, and again Jesus turned toward Jerusalem. In His heart was the peace of perfect oneness with the Father's will, and with eager steps He pressed on toward the place of sacrifice."
>
> {*Desire of Ages* 547}

"In His heart was the peace of perfect oneness with the Father's will."
I cannot conceive how a person could harmonize in his mind the
belief that while Christ's heart was in perfect oneness with the
Father's will, His will was not.

As clear as that first quote is, I believe this second quote is even
more significant, because it is taken from the chapter in *Desire of
Ages* that is based on John 5, which of course is where the statement: 'I seek not mine own will,' is found:

> "The humble Nazarene asserts His real nobility. He rises
> above humanity, throws off the guise of sin and shame, and
> stands revealed, the Honored of the angels, the Son of God,
> One with the Creator of the universe. His hearers are spell-
> bound. No man has ever spoken words like His, or borne
> himself with such a kingly majesty... Jesus repelled the
> charge of blasphemy. My authority, He said, for doing the
> work of which you accuse Me, is that I am the Son of God,
> one with Him in nature, in will, and in purpose."
>
> {*Desire of Ages* 210, 208}

According to the Spirit of Prophecy, Jesus (during one of the
greatest displays of His divinity ever given to the world) did not
say to these people: 'I *was* one with God in will', but: 'I *am* one
with God in will.' And this is the very chapter in which His words
are now being interpreted (by some) to mean the exact opposite.
I tell you: something is wrong; dreadfully wrong!

What was it that Christ was trying to tell them in those words,
'I seek not mine own will, but the will of the Father which hath
sent me?' He was trying to make them understand that in rejecting Him they were actually rejecting His Father, the God of
Abraham and Isaac and Jacob, the One whom they claimed to
believe in and of whom they claimed to be sons of. In chapter
seven He made a similar statement:

> "My doctrine is not mine, but His that sent me."
>
> {John 7:16}

Surely everyone can see that He was not saying that His
doctrine was different than His Father's; what He was saying was

that in rejecting His doctrine they were actually rejecting the Father's doctrine, whom they claimed to believe in and obey.

Now I want to begin looking at the other time Jesus made the statement, "Not my will, but thine": the garden of Gethsemane. Truly, this occasion was completely different from those first two and is worthy of the most serious consideration, as well as contemplation:

> "It would be well for us to spend a thoughtful hour each day in contemplation of the life of Christ. We should take it point by point, and let the imagination grasp each scene, *especially the closing ones*. As we thus dwell upon His great sacrifice for us, our confidence in Him will be more constant, our love will be quickened, and we shall be more deeply imbued with His spirit." {*Desire of Ages* 83}

In the attempt to clarify this point, and in keeping with that last quote, I will be quoting fairly large portions of Ellen White's account of the struggle that Jesus went through in Gethsemane. Please, take your time, and pray that God will not only show you the truth on this point, but that He will also impress upon your heart as never before, 'His great sacrifice for us.'

Was Christ's will in the garden of Gethsemane different than His Father's? Yes it was. Does this fact therefore lend validity to this teaching that Christ's will was less than perfect and that He wanted to do wrong? Absolutely not!

One extremely important thing needs to be understood and kept in mind here. That agonizing plea of Christ in Gethsemane: "*O My Father, if it be possible, let this cup pass from Me. Nevertheless not as I will, but as Thou wilt,*" was not the result of His 'wanting to do wrong'; it is exactly the opposite: it was because it was here that the plan of salvation, as well as the Father's will, called for Him to begin taking upon Himself the 'wrongs' of the entire world:

> "Christ was now standing in a different attitude from that in which He had ever stood before...Throughout His life on earth He had walked in the light of God's presence...But now He seemed to be shut out from the light of God's

sustaining presence. Now He was numbered with the transgressors. The guilt of fallen humanity He must bear. Upon Him who knew no sin must be laid the iniquity of us all. So dreadful does sin appear to Him, so great is the weight of guilt which He must bear, that He is tempted to fear it will shut Him out forever from His Father's love. Feeling how terrible is the wrath of God against transgression, He exclaims, "My soul is exceeding sorrowful, even unto death." {*Desire of Ages* 686, 685}

Was that agonizing plea: '*O My Father, if it be possible, let this cup pass from Me. Nevertheless not as I will, but as Thou wilt*', made because there was a part of Him that was being 'drawn away of His own evil desires'? Was it made because there was a part of Him that wanted to pursue a course that would take Him away from His Father? Perish the thought! That agonizing plea was made for exactly the opposite reason:

> "He felt that by sin He was being separated from His Father. The gulf was so broad, so black, so deep, that His spirit shuddered before it...The conflict was terrible...The sins of men weighed heavily upon Christ, and the sense of God's wrath against sin was crushing out His life.
>
> "Behold Him contemplating the price to be paid for the human soul. In His agony He clings to the cold ground, as if to prevent Himself from being drawn farther from God...From His pale lips comes the bitter cry, "O My Father, if it be possible, let this cup pass from Me." Yet even now He adds, "Nevertheless not as I will, but as Thou wilt."
> {*Desire of Ages* 686, 687}

> "His soul was pressed with such agony as no human being could endure and live. The sins of the world were upon him. He felt that he was separated from his Father's love; for upon him rested the curse because of sin...Human minds cannot conceive of the insupportable anguish which tortured the soul of our Redeemer."
> {*Signs of the Times*, August 14, 1879}

"We can have but faint conceptions of the inexpressible anguish of God's dear Son in Gethsemane, as He realized His separation from His Father in consequence of bearing man's sin. He became sin for the fallen race. The sense of the withdrawal of His Father's love pressed from His anguished soul these mournful words: 'My soul is exceeding sorrowful, even unto death.' 'If it be possible, let this cup pass from Me.' Then with entire submission to His Father's will, He adds: 'Nevertheless not as I will, but as Thou wilt.'

"The divine Son of God was fainting, dying."

{*2 Testimonies* 206}

In the light of all that the Spirit of Prophecy has written to help us better understand and appreciate Christ's struggle in Gethsemane, to then use those agonizing words, 'Not my will but thine', as support for the idea that there was a part of Him that wanted to do wrong, or that His will was less than perfect, is error that all Heaven must find incredibly disturbing.

Another point, a most crucial one, needs to be brought out. Those words, "Not my will, but thine", are inseparably connected to the fact that Christ was taking upon Himself the sins of the entire world. Not one of us will ever be called to take upon ourselves the sins of the world; therefore, to use those words, "Not my will, but thine", as the least justification for our will being different from God's will is a mistake of the greatest magnitude, which will lead to tragic consequences.

I would like to finish this chapter with two quotes, two questions, and two statements:

"Again the Son of God was seized with superhuman agony, and fainting and exhausted, He staggered back to the place of His former struggle."

{*Desire of Ages* 689; 'Gethsemane'}

"It was a struggle, even with the King of the universe, to yield up His Son to die for the guilty race."

{*Patriarchs and Prophets* 63}

Question #1—What caused the Son of God's struggle: was it the pull of His fallen nature, or was it "the refined sensibilities of His holy nature?"

Statement #1—When all is said and done, it will be seen that that which caused the Son of God's struggle was exactly the same as that which caused the King of the universe's struggle: a horrible realization of just how much it was going to cost to save us from sin. (Something we will spend all eternity studying.)

Question #2—Do the words, "he that hath seen Me hath seen the Father," find fulfillment even when Christ was crying out, "Not My will, but Thine"?

Statement #2—Every moment of His life Christ was revealing to all the universe the character (and love) of the Father. (Something else we will spend all eternity studying.)

Chapter 12

"WE NEED TO CONSIDER..."

Once again, it is through the Spirit of Prophecy that God has given us light and direction:

> "In the highest sense the work of education and the work of redemption are one...
>
> "In order to understand what is comprehended in the work of education, we need to consider both the nature of man and the purpose of God in creating him. We need to consider also the change in man's condition through the coming in of a knowledge of evil, and God's plan for still fulfilling His glorious purpose in the education of the human race."　　　　　　　　{*Education* 30 & 14, 15}

I would like to break this chapter into two parts. Part one is important. Part two is critical. In part one I would like to 'consider the change in man's condition through the coming in of a knowledge of evil.' In part two I would like to 'consider God's plan for still fulfilling His glorious purpose.' Both parts will be primarily a collection of quotes. Every quote (in the two groups) will contain the word 'nature'. Please read them carefully; especially the second group.

Part I—"the change in man's condition..."

"By nature the heart is evil."　　　　　{*Desire of Ages* 172}

"By nature we are alienated from God."
{*Steps to Christ* 43}

"By nature man has no love for God."
{*Review & Herald*, March 12, 1901}

"Men are selfish by nature."
{*Review & Herald*, January 6, 1891}

"The heart of man is by nature cold and dark and unloving." {*Thoughts from the Mount of Blessing* 21}

While the Spirit of Prophecy is clear that every one of us is *"born with propensities of disobedience"*, in the very same paragraph we are told just as clearly, *"Not for one moment was there in Him an evil propensity."* {*5BC* 1128} In similar manner, while it is true that, *'He took upon Him our sinful nature'*; it is also just as true that, 'not for one moment' can any of the above quotes be properly applied to Christ.

Part II—"God's plan..."

"Connected with Christ, human nature becomes pure and true." {*Messages to Young People* 35}

"As they feed upon His word, they find that it is spirit and life. The word destroys the natural, earthly nature, and imparts a new life in Christ Jesus." {*Desire of Ages* 391}

"By nature we are alienated from God... God desires to heal us, to set us free. But since this requires an entire transformation, a renewing of our whole nature, we must yield ourselves wholly to Him." {*Steps to Christ* 43}

"Every element of the nature must be purified and vitalized by the Spirit of God." {*Child Guidance* 497}

"Teach the children that because of God's great love their natures may be changed and brought into harmony with His." {*Thoughts from the Mount of Blessing* 98}

"Having taken our fallen nature, [Christ] showed what it might become..."   {*III Selected Messages* 134}

"Jesus took upon Himself man's nature, that He might leave a pattern for humanity, complete, perfect. He proposes to make us like Himself, true in every purpose, feeling, and thought—true in heart, soul, and life. This is Christianity. Our fallen nature must be purified, ennobled, consecrated by obedience to the truth."

{*5 Testimonies* 235}

"The forgiveness of sins is not the sole result of the death of Jesus. He made the infinite sacrifice, not only that sin might be removed, but that human nature might be restored, rebeautified, reconstructed from its ruins, and made fit for the presence of God."   {*5 Testimonies* 537}

In the book *Education* we are told:

"The central theme of the Bible, the theme about which every other in the whole book clusters, is the redemption plan, the restoration in the human soul of the image of God...

"He who grasps this thought...has the key that will unlock to him the whole treasure house of God's word."

{*Education* 125, 126}

In like manner, he (or she) who not only grasps the thought, but has written in his heart and fulfilled in his life the truths contained in that last series of quotes, will have the key that will unlock to him the answer to this whole question. He will not only know in head knowledge, but infinitely more important, he will know by experience, that 'the man Christ Jesus,' the man of whom it is written,

"For there stood in the world One who was a perfect representative of the Father."   {*I Selected Messages* 254}

was never 'drawn away of His own lust,' neither was He 'drawn away of His own evil desires.'

Chapter 13

"HIS SOUL'S SALVATION IS AT STAKE..."

If there is any subject that could rightly be called a 'two-edged sword', this next one is it.

God in His infinite wisdom and love has made it clear that the ministry can be the greatest of blessings; or, it can be the greatest of curses.

Because this point is so important, while also being such a delicate issue, I will refrain from adding any of my own thoughts; instead, I will simply share a selection of inspired quotes. Some of them will set before us the sacredness and blessedness of the true minister of God; others will set before us our need to be exceeding careful. I will break them into two groups:

Group #1:

"There is nothing more precious in the sight of God than His ministers."   {*Acts of the Apostles* 369}

"To the physician equally with the gospel minister is committed the highest trust ever committed to man."
{*Ministry of Healing* 119}

"The minister stands as God's mouthpiece to the people."   {*Gospel Workers* 20}

"Since His ascension, Christ the great Head of the church, has carried forward His work in the world by chosen ambassadors, through whom He speaks to the children of men, and ministers to their needs."
{*Gospel Workers* 13}

"The sweet influences that are to be abundant in the church are bound up with God's ministers..."

{*Acts of the Apostles* 586}

"It is hardly possible for men to offer greater insult to God than to despise and reject the instrumentalities He would use for their salvation." {*Patriarchs and Prophets* 402}

Group #2:

"O my people, they which lead thee cause thee to err."

{Isaiah 3:12}

"For the rejection of Christ, with the results that followed, they were responsible. A nation's sin and a nation's ruin were due to the religious leaders."

{*Christ's Object Lessons* 305}

"As the light and life of men was rejected by the ecclesiastical authorities in the days of Christ, so it has been rejected in every succeeding generation." {*Desire of Ages* 232}

"The church will rarely take a higher stand than is taken by her ministers." {*5 Testimonies* 227}

"Parents are not to trust their own souls and the souls of their children to the minister, but to God, whose they are by creation and by redemption. Parents should search the Scriptures for themselves, for they have souls to save or to lose. They cannot afford to depend for salvation upon the minister. They must study the truth for themselves."

{*Child Guidance* 513}

"It becomes us to be diligent Bible students, that we may know what is according to the law and the testimony. We are safe in no other course of action."

{*II Selected Messages* 99}

"HIS SOUL'S SALVATION IS AT STAKE..."

"It is not enough to do what a man thinks is right or what the minister tells him is right. His soul's salvation is at stake, and he should search the Scriptures for himself. However strong may be his convictions, however confident he may be that the minister knows what is truth, this is not his foundation...With divine help we are to form our opinions for ourselves as we are to answer for ourselves before God."

{*Great Controversy* 598}

Chapter 14

"FINALLY BRETHREN"

I would like to spend the majority of this final chapter examining two points. #1: The importance of this subject in the over-all scheme of things. And, #2: The importance of perfect obedience.

Point #1—The importance of this subject

I want to begin with two quotes, that when considered together cannot fail to raise some very serious questions:

"The shaking must soon take place to purify the church."
{*II Spiritual Gifts* 284}

"The mighty shaking has commenced and will go on…"
{*Early Writings* 50}

It has been over a hundred years since those words were written. Multitudes from all walks of life are praying and working and waiting for the church to be purified. Multitudes are doing their best to live by these words:

"Mark this point with care: Those who receive the pure mark of truth, wrought in them by the power of the Holy Ghost, represented by a mark by the man in linen, are those "that sigh and that cry for all the abominations that be done" in the church."   {*3 Testimonies* 267}

And multitudes, with greater and greater perplexity:

"Cry with a loud voice, saying, How long O Lord."
{Revelation 6:9, 10}

To all there comes back one all-important answer:

> "Christ is waiting with longing desire for the manifestation of Himself in His church. When the character of Christ shall be perfectly reproduced in His people, then He will come to claim them as His own." {*Christ's Object Lessons* 69}

The doctrinal truths that we as Seventh-day Adventists have been given are precious and indispensable. (Though many are doing their best to dispense with them.) They are truths that we must do all in our power to make known to the world. They are truths, the reception or rejection of which will determine the destiny of souls. But they are truths that will prove themselves absolutely powerless to solve our problems if not combined with knowing Christ and possessing His character:

> "Christ, his character and work, is the center and circumference of all truth, he is the chain upon which the jewels of doctrine are linked. In him is found the complete system of truth…The business of every Christian is to study the character of Christ." {*Review & Herald*, August 15, 1893}
> {*That I May Know Him*, Chapter 176}

> "Though I have the [Spirit] of prophecy, and understand all mysteries, and all knowledge…and have not [Christ], I am nothing." {I Corinthians 13:2}

> "To know God and Christ—this is eternal life. Incorporated with the life, this knowledge fits us for heaven. And all other knowledge, however high or broad, unless charged with it, is valueless in God's sight." {*I Sermons and Talks* 334}

If we understand and are able to explain with perfect clearness the Sabbath, the State of the Dead, the Sanctuary, and every other great truth that God has made known to this people, but fail to bear a likeness to Christ in character, we will one day hear those saddest of all words:

"Depart from Me, I never knew you." {Matthew 7:23}

And, as disturbing a thought as it may be, it is entirely possible to practice health reform, dress reform, and every other reform that is found in the Spirit of Prophecy (all of which are as indispensable as our doctrines), and yet still, because we do not truly have Christ formed within, be found in that awful condition described in those words of Christ Himself:

> "Ye are like unto whited sepulchres, which indeed appear beautiful outward, but are within full of dead men's bones, and of all uncleanness. Even so ye also outwardly appear righteous unto men, but within ye are full of hypocrisy and iniquity." {Matthew 23:27, 28}

Undoubtedly, there are an almost endless number of important Spirit of Prophecy quotes; but there are two that demand to be exalted just now:

> "The humanity of the Son of God is everything to us. It is the golden chain that binds our souls to Christ, and through Christ to God. This is to be our study."
> {*I Selected Messages* 244}

> "One question will be all absorbing—Who shall approach the nearest to the likeness of Christ?"
> {*General Conference Daily Bulletin,* February 6, 1893}

There is another factor in this whole question that we cannot afford to be unmindful of—Satan:

> "Notwithstanding the infinite power and majesty of God and Christ, angels became disaffected. The insinuations of Satan took effect, and they really came to believe that the Father and the Son were their enemies and that Satan was their benefactor. Satan has the same power and the same control over minds now, only it has increased a hundredfold by exercise and experience." {*3 Testimonies* 328}

"[Lucifer] sought to gain control of heavenly beings, to draw them away from their Creator, and to win their homage to himself. *Therefore* he misrepresented God…With his own evil characteristics he sought to invest the loving Creator. *Thus* he deceived angels. *Thus* he deceived men."

{*Desire of Ages* 21, 22}

Satan is pursuing a similar course today, only this time it is the Son instead of the Father that he is misrepresenting; and he is having just as much success as he did thousands of years ago. I have seen 'the man Christ Jesus', the One of whom we have read was 'Infinite Purity', the One who said of Himself, 'he that hath seen Me hath seen the Father,' portrayed as not only being 'drawn away of His own lust', and 'drawn away of His own evil desires', but having to battle inwardly with such traits as pride, selfishness, and unholy ambition. This is no less than a perfect fulfillment of those words:

"With his own evil characteristics he sought to invest the loving Creator."   {*Desire of Ages* 22}

Let me finish this section by saying that after a great deal of prayer (and much struggle) it seemed clear to me that it would be best not to mention any names. I cannot help but be convinced that naming names would do far more harm than it would good. I will only repeat what I said in chapter one: very few people seem to realize just how serious and just how wide-spread this problem actually is.

Point #2—The importance of perfect obedience

Perfect obedience is a teaching that for the majority of old-fashioned, conservative Seventh-day Adventists is neither new nor questionable; which only makes failure to live up to it infinitely more serious. Failure on this point will make it impossible for us to ever reproduce the character of Christ. And it is failure on this point that is ultimately behind so many other problems.

As is the case with so many subjects, we are once again brought back to a statement I made earlier: "this question of the exact place that God designs the Spirit of Prophecy to occupy in the life (and heart) of every true Seventh-day Adventist."

Once again I ask you to consider what God has done in giving to us the writings of Ellen White:

> "One stood by my side and said: 'God has raised you up and has given you words to speak to the people and to reach hearts as He has given to no other one.'" {*2 Testimonies* 607}

Try to realize that if the words she was given to speak to us do not reach our hearts to the point where we long for entire conformity to the will of God then there is very little left that He can do:

> "I saw that the judgments of the Almighty were speedily coming, and I begged of the angel to speak in his language to the people. Said he, "All the thunders and lightnings of Mount Sinai would not move those who will not be moved by the plain truths of the Word of God, neither would an angel's message awake them." {*Early Writings* 50}

In a few minutes I will be sharing some very 'plain truths' on the subject of perfect obedience. I pray that they will 'reach hearts' as never before. But before doing that I would like to lay some groundwork.

Since the heart is such an essential element in 'reaching hearts', I would like to share two quotes concerning it. The first is a portion of a quote I used earlier. Please, do not allow its shortness and simplicity to cause you to underestimate its importance. The second quote is probably one of the most important quotes in this entire book:

> "All true obedience comes from the heart."
> {*Desire of Ages* 668}

> "Men will never be truly temperate until the grace of Christ is an abiding principle in the heart. All the pledges in the world will not make you or your wife health reformers. No mere restriction of your diet will cure your diseased

appetite. Brother and Sister ———- will not practice temperance in all things until their hearts are transformed by the grace of God.

"...The plan of beginning outside and trying to work inward has always failed, and always will fail. God's plan with you is to begin at the very seat of all difficulties, the heart..." {*Counsels on Diet and Foods* 35}

That last sentence, and I re-quote it because it deserves to be re-quoted, "God's plan with you (and me) is to begin at the very seat of all difficulties, the heart...", contains one of the greatest truths in all the Christian religion. Please, stop for a minute, and pray that God will magnify this truth to you as never before, and pray that you will realize as never before that your very salvation (not to mention all those whom God may design to reach through you) will be determined by how you react to this one truth.

Next I want to share two extremely solemn quotes that once again make unmistakably clear the importance of the *Testimonies*:

"Perilous times are before us. Everyone who has a knowledge of the truth should awake and place himself, body, soul, and spirit, under the discipline of God. The enemy is on our track. We must be wide awake, on our guard against him. We must put on the whole armor of God. We must follow the directions given through the spirit of prophecy. We must love and obey the truth for this time. This will save us from accepting strong delusions. God has spoken to us through His word. He has spoken to us through the testimonies to the church and through the books that have helped to make plain our present duty and the position that we should now occupy. The warnings that have been given, line upon line, precept upon precept, should be heeded. If we disregard them, what excuse can we offer?"

{*8 Testimonies* 298}

"Testimonies of warning have been repeated. I inquire: Who have heeded them? Who have been zealous in repenting of their sins and idolatry, and have been earnestly pressing toward the mark for the prize of the high calling of God in Christ Jesus?...I have waited anxiously, hoping that God would put His Spirit upon some and use them as instruments of righteousness to awaken and set in order His church. I have almost despaired as I have seen, year after year, a greater departure from that simplicity which God has shown me should characterize the life of His followers. There has been less and less interest in, and devotion to, the cause of God. I ask: Wherein have those who profess confidence in the Testimonies sought to live according to the light given in them? Wherein have they regarded the warnings given? Wherein have they heeded the instructions they have received?"   {*2 Testimonies* 483, 484}
{*5 Testimonies* 662, 663}

Those last two quotes, as solemn as they are, are very general; yet we read earlier, *"Your testimony is to come down to the minutiae of life."*{*5T* 667} So now I would like to look at a few quotes that address one specific subject. As we look at these quotes I pray more than anything that God will impress upon your hearts the reality that the specific subject that I am about to look at is just one in a multitude of subjects in which her testimony is to come down to the minutiae of life; and that every word, concerning every subject, is *"the solemn testimony upon which [our] destiny hangs"* {*EW* 270}; and that every word is *"but the breathing of unutterable love."*{*SC* 35} Please, as you read these quotes, pray that God will help you to correctly apply this principle of her writings coming down to the minutiae of life to whatever area of your own life that it might need to be applied to.

I will begin by repeating a portion of one of those more general quotes:

"I have waited anxiously... I have almost despaired... I ask: Wherein have those who profess confidence in the Testimonies sought to live according to the light given in them?"   {*2 Testimonies* 484} {*5 Testimonies* 663}

"Many who profess to believe the Testimonies live in neglect of the light given. The dress reform is treated by some with great indifference and by others with contempt, because there is a cross attached to it. For this cross I thank God. It is just what we need to distinguish and separate God's commandment-keeping people from the world. The dress reform answers to us as did the ribbon of blue to ancient Israel." {*3 Testimonies* 171}

"Not one in twenty of the sisters who profess to believe the Testimonies has taken the first step in the dress reform." {*1 Testimonies* 465}

"Do not, my sisters, trifle longer with your own souls and with God...Obedience to fashion is pervading our Seventh-day Adventist churches and is doing more than any other power to separate our people from God." {*4 Testimonies* 647}

I would like to point out one more thing before sharing those quotes on perfect obedience. To me it is crucial. We are told:

"Man shall not live by bread alone but by *every* word that proceeds out of the mouth of God." {Matthew 4:4}

"*All* His words are spirit and life. Accepted and obeyed, they will give peace and happiness and assurance forever." {*Review & Herald*, April 12, 1892} {*Our High Calling*, chapter 323}

"God has declared that man's only means of safety is entire obedience to *all* His words." {*Conflict and Courage*, chapter 14}

As you read through these quotes you will see phrases such as: '*perfect and entire* obedience', '*exact* obedience', '*unswerving* obedience', '*any* known sin', '*a* known sin', etc. Please, pray as never

before that you will truly understand that every single word
means exactly what it says:

"The law of God will be satisfied with nothing short of
perfection, of perfect and entire obedience to all its claims.
To come halfway to its requirements, and not render
perfect and thorough obedience, will avail nothing."

{*1 Testimonies* 416}

"Never, till exemplified in the sacrifice of Christ, were
the justice and the love of God more strikingly displayed
than in His dealings with Moses. God shut Moses out of
Canaan, to teach a lesson which should never be forgotten—that He requires exact obedience."

{*Patriarchs and Prophets* 479}

"The law demands perfect, unswerving obedience...Men
are weighed in the balance and found wanting when they
are living in the practice of any known sin...Let no one
deceive his own soul in this matter."

{*Testimonies to Ministers* 440, 441}

"Let none deceive themselves with the belief that they
can become holy while willfully violating one of God's
requirements. The commission of a known sin silences the
witnessing voice of the Spirit and separates the soul from
God." {*Great Controversy* 392}

"He who willfully breaks one commandment, does not,
in spirit and truth, keep any of them... It is not the greatness
of the act of disobedience that constitutes sin, but the fact of
variance from God's expressed will in the least particular...
Not by one word, not by many words, but by every word
that God has spoken, shall man live. We cannot disregard
one word, however trifling it may seem to us, and be safe.
There is not a commandment of the law that is not for the
good and happiness of man, both in this life and in the life to
come. In obedience to God's law, man is surrounded as

with a hedge and kept from the evil. He who breaks down this divinely erected barrier at one point has destroyed its power to protect him; for he has opened a way by which the enemy can enter to waste and ruin.

"By venturing to disregard the will of God upon one point, our first parents opened the floodgates of woe upon the world. And every individual who follows their example will reap a similar result. The love of God underlies every precept of His law, and he who departs from the commandment is working his own unhappiness and ruin."

{ Thoughts from the Mount of Blessing 51, 52}

"We cannot overestimate the value of simple faith and unquestioning obedience. It is by following in the path of obedience in simple faith that the character obtains perfection."
{ 4 Bible Commentary 1137}

"One safeguard removed from conscience, the indulgence of one evil habit, a single neglect of the high claims of duty, may be the beginning of a course of deception that will pass you into the ranks of those who are serving Satan, while you are all the time professing to love God and His cause."
{ 5 Testimonies 398}

Conclusion

Theological discussions will go on till the end of time; and they certainly have a place and a purpose. But theological discussions are not what we need most to come to a knowledge of the truth:

"If we ever know the truth, it will be because we practice it."
{ Counsels to Parents and Teachers 97}

In closing, Inspiration tells us:

"O how love I thy law! It is my meditation all the day."
{ Psalms 119:97}

"Fill the whole heart with the words of God. They are the living water, quenching your burning thirst. They are the living bread from heaven...It is what we meditate upon that will give tone and strength to our spiritual nature."

{*Steps to Christ* 88}

"There is life in God's word...He who by faith receives the word is receiving the very life and character of God."

{*Christ's Object Lessons* 38}

Please, more than anything else: cultivate loving God. This begins and centers in cultivating a love for every single word He has spoken to us.

"The man who cherishes the most of Christ's love in the soul, who reflects the Saviour's image most perfectly, is in the sight of God the truest, most noble, most honorable man upon the earth."

{*5 Testimonies* 235}